WHERE THE BRAVE DARE NOT GO

Lela Gilbert

WHERE THE BRAVE DARE NOT GO
Copyright © 2016 by Friends in the West
ISBN: 978-0-9973668-0-8

All RIGHTS RESERVED
No part of this book may be reproduced in any form – electronic, mechanical, or with any other means, including photocopying – without the author's written permission, except in the case of brief quotations embodied in critical articles or reviews.

Written by Lela Gilbert
Cover Design by Mike Thorpe
Book Formatting by Hydra House

Published by Friends in the West
www.friendsinthewest.com

First Printing 1987

Walk, with your head bent in sorrow,
run where the brave dare not go.

Because their love and support has meant so much to Ray, I would like to dedicate this book to his family: Ruth, Rob, Rheanne and Rhonda.

Ray and I would like to acknowledge all the faithful Friends in the West who have prayed behind the scenes for over fifteen years.

I would also like to offer special thanks to my friend Lila Fulton who so faithfully prayed for me as I wrote this book.

—Lela Gilbert

CONTENTS

- 7   FOREWORD
- 9   PREFACE
- 11   ONE | MESSENGER TO TURBULENT BEIRUT
- 16   TWO | THE YOUNG DREAMER FINDS A NEW DREAM
- 27   THREE | STRANGE FACES EXCITING PLACES
- 40   FOUR | ROCKY BEGINNINGS
- 48   FIVE | SIGNS AND WONDERS FROM GOD
- 58   SIX | FAITH AT WORK IN WASHINGTON
- 70   SEVEN | MIRACLES IN AFRICA AND BERLIN
- 79   EIGHT | AMAZING ANSWERS TO PRAYER
- 89   NINE | CLANDESTINE CAMPING TRIP TO MOSCOW
- 98   TEN | SUFFERING AND RELIEF IN THE MIDDLE EAST
- 109   ELEVEN | EXTRAORDINARY PRAYERS AND PROMISES
- 118   TWELVE | WONDROUS THINGS HAPPEN EVERY DAY
- 128   EPILOGUE | FEBRUARY 2016

FOREWORD

How does one describe Ray Barnett? St. Augustine once said, "Pray as though everything depended on God. Work as though everything depended on you." This is Ray—a man whose tireless efforts are done without fanfare, without publicity. Some men seek fame and fortune. Ray Barnett simply seeks freedom for those who have lost their human rights.

This is the story of an orphan who found his mother and sister through a miracle—who went on to reach out to other needy orphans in other parts of the world.

This is the story of a youth whose stuttering was cured by prayer—who went on to speak out boldly on behalf of persecuted people and those held against their will.

This is the story of a man who has been invisibly responsible for both prayers and practical efforts resulting in freedom for men, women, and children throughout the world. His work goes on even today.

My family and I continue to be grateful for the loving efforts made by Ray Barnett and Friends in the West during my captivity. And I applaud his ongoing endeavours as he brings to life the words of Scripture found in Hebrews 13:3: "Remember those in prison as if you were imprisoned with them."

—David Jacobsen, 1987

PREFACE

Like a kaleidoscope of stained-glass images, my childhood memories are colorfully patterned with church music, Sunday school lessons and ten thousand long-forgotten sermons. A sawdust aisle led the way to the revival-tent altar where I first "accepted Jesus" into my child's heart.

There were baptisms. Church suppers. Communion services. Easter cantatas. Bible passages were evaluated from every possible perspective. Old and New Testament miracles alike were soundly defended theologically.

Everyone agreed. Those signs and wonders all happened just the way the Good Book said they did-two thousand years ago.

When I started to research Ray Barnett's unique adventures, I was already wondering why the power had been removed from "the power and the glory." Where had it gone? Why had God Almighty changed His style just when mankind needed His supernatural intervention more desperately than ever?

Each episode in this book was carefully examined. One by one, the various characters were interviewed. I waited to hear just one person say, "Well, that's really not quite the way it was. Don't get carried away with that spiritual stuff."

Instead I heard much the opposite. "Is that all He told you? It I was certainly more dramatic than that!"

Today I stand fully convinced. Every event described in this book is true—beyond the shadow of a doubt. God IS continuing to break through into our earthbound, everyday lives. Just as He I did in ancient sacred histories, He persists in revealing Himself as a loving, caring Heavenly Father who is quite capable of doing exactly as He pleases. And He still takes delight in answering our prayers.

To my immense personal relief and rejoicing, the age of miracles has not passed.

—Lela Gilbert, Lake Arrowhead, California, 1987

ONE

MESSENGER TO TURBULENT BEIRUT

Tension gripped the August night in 1986 as the Cypriate authorities completed their security check. Once they were satisfied that Ray Barnett was not on a mission of smuggling or sabotage, he would be moved along into another area to be searched and inspected by Lebanese customs and immigration control.

Ray was on his way from Cyprus into Beirut. Since the Beirut airport had become so dangerous for Westerners, he was about to board a small ship that carried passengers across the Mediterranean into that beleaguered city.

The well-worn but comfortable vessel even featured its own gambling casino. Passengers quickly found their way to the slot machines, and the jangle of coins dulled their unspoken awareness of danger.

Ray walked to his cabin and absently put his belongings away. "At least it's not as hot as it was last year." He recalled the stifling air of that May, 1985, voyage. As it turned out, that was the very time when David Jacobsen, administrator of the American University Hospital of Beirut, had been kidnapped. Now Ray was returning to Lebanon to see what he could do on behalf of Jacobsen and his fellow hostages.

In 1982, when Ray had worked in Lebanon during the Israeli invasion, he had developed a number of close friendships there. His relief efforts had provided food and medical assistance for the war-ravaged people in southern Lebanon. This had endeared him to many, including well-respected Shia Muslims. Now he would contact those friends on behalf of the American hostages. He would initiate a concerted prayer effort. He would also try to learn what he could about the captive Americans' circumstances.

He rubbed his eyes and stretched out across the bunk. "By the time I wake up," he promised himself, "I'll be in Beirut." And so he was. He headed again for the customs inspection area.

"What is this, platinum? Silver?"

A sharp-eyed customs official pulled a bag of silver-tone bracelets from Ray's bag. He studied them carefully, his face animated—maybe this was a real find. But why the names on all the bracelets?

TERRY ANDERSON, March 16, 1985
THOMAS SUTHERLAND, June 9, 1985
DAVID JACOBSEN, May 18, 1985

"No," Ray chuckled, somewhat amused by the question. "They aren't silver or platinum. They're aluminum or some other kind of inexpensive metal. They're prayer bracelets."

Filled with questions, the man's brown eyes looked into Ray's. "Prayer bracelets?"

"Yes," Ray nodded. "They have the names of America's hostages in Lebanon on them. And look ... " He squeezed the bracelets on his wrist to demonstrate the softness of the metal. "You can't bend platinum or silver that easily!"

"Then they aren't valuable?"

Ray paused for a moment, considering the question. In fifteen years, many names had been inscribed on prayer bracelets—and millions of people had prayed, reminded to do so by the bracelets. So far every imprisoned person whose name had ever appeared on a Friends in the West prayer bracelet had eventually been released from captivity.

"Valuable?" he smiled. "Not a bit valuable in financial terms. But ..." He left the sentence unfinished as he was motioned to move on. Once again, he had cleared customs.

Setting Up the Network

Soon a taxi was rushing him to the Hotel Alexandre, which had continued to do business despite countless bombings. There he set up an informal base of operations and began his efforts. Most of the contacts he made were with members of Beirut's Muslim community. The hotel's location was practical because of its proximity to the infamous Green Line, which divided the city into Christian and Muslim sectors.

His primary liaison was a man who had become a committed Christian during the 1982 relief effort. This man's business kept him deeply involved with Lebanon's Muslim people, and his ties with the diplomatic community gave him invaluable insights into potential avenues of assistance for the hostages.

This Lebanese gentleman and his wife insisted that Ray meet His Beatitude Patriarch Maximus Five Hakim, a world-famous religious leader. He was international head over the Greek Catholic church, and Ray's friends felt that he had a certain voice within the Syrian government. Since there were those who insisted that the Syrian government had unofficial influence with the kidnappers of the Americans, an audience with Hakim seemed imperative.

Ray Barnett glanced at himself in the hotel room mirror as he prepared for his meeting with the Patriarch. He stopped and ran his fingers absently through his dark brown hair. Cleaning his glasses he smiled to himself. "I've made so many trips like this in my life ... into the Soviet Union. Uganda. Eastern Europe. Mozambique. I always feel the Lord has sent me. But I never know what to expect. Now here I am again ... "

He was introduced to Patriarch Hakim, finding himself in the presence of a diminutive, white-bearded man of more than ninety years. His place in the Middle Eastern religious community was legendary. The serene priest was deeply moved by Ray's appeal for prayer. He later made a public statement, which was published throughout that part of the world:

Recently the President of the Hostage Crisis Prayer Campaign contacted us to pray with the American people for the release of the hostages. And we have realized that we have underestimated the power of prayer ... for through prayer, God will mediate with the kidnappers and His power will overwhelm any human authority.

One by one, Ray was introduced to leaders of the Shia Muslim community. Doctors met with him—doctors who knew David Jacobsen as a hospital administrator.

"He is a fine man," one of them told Ray. "I will personally do anything and everything I can to work toward his release." The doctors agreed to try to set aside a day of prayer at the hospital. David Jacobsen bracelets were taken into West Beirut and distributed among the hospital's medical staff.

Ray felt somewhat satisfied with the progress he was making. He had brought the hostage problem into the open through his channels in Beirut. Prayer meetings were organized. Quiet, social conversations would communicate concern for the Americans back into the Shia community. But just before Ray left, one last introduction was made.

One Last Meeting

The man was brought to the hotel by a mutual friend. He was shaken when he arrived.

"The man who crossed the Green Line just behind me was shot dead!"

The three men talked. "I grew up in a village near Baalbek," the Shia Muslim businessman explained. "The leaders of the Islamic Jihad are people that I've known most of my life."

"I've met David Jacobsen's sons," Ray told him. Genuine compassion burned in the man's eyes as Ray quietly spoke.

"Eric, his oldest son, had spent months of his life working for his father's release. He and his brother Paul have written and recorded a beautiful song about David Jacobsen's captivity. Like Terry Anderson's sister, Peggy Say, they've done so many American television and radio interviews that they can't count them. They are all wonderful people and their hearts have been broken by these kidnappings. I want to help them."

The Muslim shook his head sadly. "I don't know how much good it will do. But I'll go up to Baalbek and I'll see what I can find out."

Next evening, Ray boarded the boat for his return home. As he stood on the deck watching moonlight dancing across the waters, he reviewed his four days in Beirut.

"Lord," he prayed silently, "I've been in this situation a thousand times before. It's always been the same—I sense Your direction, I obey You, and then I have to wait for You to accomplish the rest.

"As far as this hostage effort is concerned, we're absolutely helpless without You. Please guide me—let me know what You want me to do next. And be with the others—the Patriarch, the Muslim doctors, the young man from Baalbek.

"I know You led me to try and help these hostages, and I'm nothing more than a messenger of Your love. But for now I've done all I can think of. *You'll* have to do the rest. Just like always ... "

TWO

THE YOUNG DREAMER FINDS A NEW DREAM

The day in early October, 1936, dawned clear and crisp. Across the choppy waters, a distant peninsula dozed peacefully in the Irish morning. Life began to stir in the simple, weather-beaten dwellings blown by a never ceasing wind.

Young Bob Letson timidly let himself out of the maternity home, closing the door as he went. The North Atlantic roared wildly just a block away, thundering against the beach that curved toward Castlerock.

Bob glanced down at the remarkably small infant he held in his arms, wrapped as warmly as possible in a woolen shawl. He felt embarrassed and awkward. Was anyone watching?

"Everyone says there's not a chance in the world you'll live," he gently spoke to the sleeping baby. "But I'm going to do what I can for you."

The infant was just ten days old. He had weighed barely three and a half pounds at birth. To everyone's amazement, he was still breathing. But his body was scrawny and his color pale and lifeless. "It's a wonder Lavina Ross is willing to take you in. She's already got more than enough children of her own."

The young father turned toward the town of Coleraine, the damp wind pushing against his back. Now the boy began to stir and cry. His tiny voice was almost soundless, but it greatly disturbed Bob. He felt more fearful than ever. "Please don't die!" he said hoarsely. "We've got nearly six miles to go."

At last he arrived at a small Ulster cottage set on a hill above the gently winding River Bann. The sea was well behind him now, and from the hilltop he could see tidy fields and hedgerows ripening into autumn hues. He stopped briefly and watched the river wind its way toward the North Atlantic.

A New Home

Lavina Ross's friendly face stood behind the open cottage door. She immediately took the baby from Bob, her smile fading a bit at the sight of his fragile body.

Lavina knew all about babies. When her mother died she was forced to leave school at ten years of age to care for her many younger brothers and sisters. And now, after marrying James, she had seven surviving children of her own. Two others had died early in their lives.

"Sit down and I'll put on the tea," she said to Bob. Her voice was reassuring and calm. She'd already tucked the little boy into a well-worn cradle, and he was sleeping peacefully. Bob felt himself beginning to relax.

Not long after Bob Letson's departure, Lavina summoned the family doctor. He examined the infant carefully, a concerned look in his eyes. Finally he shrugged, "Let him reign short or let him reign long. Why don't you call him Raymond?"

Days passed. Lavina fed him warm milk, and soon a week was gone. Then a fortnight. Then a month. And still he breathed. At two months he was baptized Robert Raymond Ross at St. Patrick's Church that presides over the bustling Coleraine marketplace.

To the wonder of all except perhaps Mrs. Ross herself, the boy appeared to be a survivor. And as for Lavina, she had spent countless hours beside him, struggling along with him night and day, sharing his battle for life. Now, as she watched him receive the formal blessing of God at the baptismal font, she recognized that a gentle, powerful love was growing in her heart. There was something almost miraculous about this tenacious little blue-eyed fighter.

Who was he meant to be? Where was he meant to go? Many years would pass before those questions were answered. Meanwhile, little Raymond grew stronger and older. Before long Lavina was preparing him to go to school.

Problems in the Classroom

For an institutional structure, the single-story primary school was a pleasant enough place. A large communal garden thrived near the play area. Children's happy voices filled the air with laughter and carefree chatter.

Raymond Ross sat in the corner of the school yard, nibbling at the lunch his older sister had brought to him. He absently ate the sandwich and drank the small container of tea, watching the other children at play. He knew that he was different from the boys and girls around him. But he wasn't sure why.

The classroom had already proved to be a troublesome setting for the small, somewhat frail child of seven. Why was the schoolwork so difficult for him? The teacher, nice as she was, had begun the year harping at him for daydreaming. And by now it seemed that she had more or less stopped trying to teach him.

His problems had begun with arithmetic sums. They had carried over into writing, where the letters never seemed to look quite the way they were intended. And, of course, there was the halt in his speech—words came out backwards. Upside down. Or, worse yet, they didn't come out at all.

In those uncertain, violent days of 1942, war with Germany was pounding full force against the British Isles. Telegrams were delivered daily to the quiet Ulster community, reporting the death of a father. Or a brother. Or a young husband. The school windows were criss-crossed with tape to prevent the glass from splintering in a bombing raid. And even the smallest, poorest child in town carried a gas mask to class in case of enemy attack.

These were not times when special children were given special attention. In fact the very opposite was true. Teachers were in short supply. Good, wise teachers were rare as gold. And words like "learning disabled" were yet to enter the vocabulary of the English-speaking world.

So "wee Raymond Ross" was categorized, along with scores of similar children around the globe, as a boy who seemed a bit simpleminded. And yet there was one curious fact that contradicted that conclusion: Raymond could read. And he could read remarkably well.

One dreary afternoon early in the school year he sat humiliated as the arithmetic lesson continued. In no way could he grasp the figures, or give the proper answers. And so, before five minutes had passed, his mind had left the many-windowed classroom and taken him far away. In his world of dreams he was marvelously free.

But soon the subject changed. The miserable numbers were put away. In their place came a time of reading aloud. Unexpectedly, the teacher called on Raymond. He stood up, book in hand. And he read. Perfectly. Clearly. Without the slightest hesitation in his speech.

The teacher was puzzled. She had little time to contemplate the variety of young students that crossed her path everyday. And she was ill-equipped to deal with out-of-the-ordinary handicaps. But this was perplexing. How was it Raymond could read so well? And what was it in his eyes? Something told her he was anything but dim-witted.

Still, in spite of his rare triumphs, school was not a particularly appealing place to young Raymond. He used any creative opportunity available to avoid going. Walking alone in the glorious, green countryside around Coleraine was far more suitable for dreaming than under the critical eye of his teacher.

Lavina Ross knew that her adopted boy was a unique child. And she also knew that school was a burden to him. She kept a close eye on him, quick to determine that, from time to time, he was scheming to stay home. This required a great deal of discernment on her part for Raymond was still a sickly child.

Meanwhile, his lack of physical coordination limited him in play. He just couldn't catch the ball. He simply could not accomplish the feats by which children challenge and compete with one another. He was even unable to tell his right foot from his left.

If playground participation was difficult, music was a nightmare. One day during band rehearsal, his bandmaster gave Raymond two shiny cymbals. "Just keep time with the music, that's all you have to do." He might as well have asked him to fly to the moon. The noise was dreadful.

"How about a triangle?" he suggested kindly, passing the clanging cymbal to a more rhythmic child. The result was quieter but no less chaotic.

Some years later part of Raymond's music class formed a choir and began to rehearse a performance. He was terrified. He stood near the top of the little group choking with fear. Before the first trembling words could cross his lips he felt himself tingling. Weakening. Within a few paralyzing seconds he had completely lost consciousness.

A New Confidence

By now most of his teachers were ready to give up on the boy. "Look, Raymond," the young music teacher quietly spoke to him after class. "I can see that music is not something you enjoy. Can you read?" She looked somewhat skeptical when he mutely nodded. "You can? Good. Then you may read during music class."

He was ecstatic! He sat at a small wooden desk devouring the books that miraculously carried him away from the classroom's tensions and traumas. One afternoon the young teacher glanced at the cover of Raymond's book. She took a second look. Could he really be reading that? It was a difficult book, a complicated one.

As discreetly as possible she tried to quiz the boy about the story. Every answer was accurate. She shook her head, studying the boy's intense, clear eyes. There were so many things he couldn't do. Yet he was reading years and years ahead of himself.

As kind as she was curious, she invited Raymond to her home on certain afternoons. She began to work with him, to try as best she could to sort out the complexities of his young mind. She helped him struggle through his sums. She guided him as he desperately tried to write words with all the letters turned the right way.

But it wasn't the woman's teaching that began to change Raymond's life. It was her interest. It inspired him. Someone else besides Lavina saw some potential in him. He knew it was there. And now this concerned teacher knew it was there too. Yet the question haunted him—what would he ever be able to do with his life?

One springtime afternoon in his eleventh year found Raymond intently studying a map of North America. A deep longing held him spellbound. Uncommon names, unimaginable places—they filled him with a yearning he could barely fathom.

The name of a western Canadian waterway particularly caught his eye. "The Fraser River ... " he whispered to himself. A quiet smile curved his lips. His shining eyes wandered past the classroom windows, past the lush greenery outside to a wild, open land he could hardly envision.

The Fraser River. Canada. The words flooded his heart with hope. "I expect I'll be going there someday. I don't know how I'll do it. But I will."

A New Dream

Raymond's goal to someday see western Canada was all the more wild in light of his adoptive family's financial situation. The Ross's were big-hearted people, and their children were well cared for. But the older children had to help out as much as possible. Once Raymond reached his eleventh year he began taking whatever job he could, wherever he could find it.

By fourteen, he'd worked for nearly half the shopkeepers in Coleraine. Like other youngsters, he was paid a coin or two each week for delivering goods from marketplace to customer. It certainly wasn't much of an income. But with a family as large as James Ross's, every shilling counted.

Raymond never walked slowly. But one day his already quick feet seemed to have wings on them. He had his eye on yet another target for employment. There was a photography studio in town. Perhaps he could work there. He needed a new job, and something about photography intrigued him.

The studio was located at the top of a staircase not far from the busiest part of town. Raymond knocked on the door and a kind-faced woman answered. Wording his request with care to avoid hopelessly stumbling over his own question, the boy politely inquired, "Would you have any work I could do for you?"

Had they noticed his difficulty in speaking? Almost without breathing he watched them as they glanced at each other. Something unspoken seemed to pass between them.

"Yes," the photographer said, looking rather unsure as to what he was about to do. "Yes ... I think we can put you to work." His wife nodded with an approving smile and left the room.

Raymond was so pleased with his good fortune that he didn't take the time to guess whether the couple had suddenly created a job for him. He would begin tomorrow.

The work proved to be most interesting. Besides his usual delivery chores, he occasionally had the opportunity to assist in the darkroom. The acrid smells and the fascinating process of film development and printing appealed to him.

And he soon discovered that there was more going on at the studio than photography. The gentleman who'd hired Raymond seemed to be a part-time preacher as well as a camera buff. A new sort of people came and went, different in their conversation from the average townspeople.

One day as he worked, the boy heard his boss, Jim Dunlop, and a friend discussing an unusual subject—missionaries. Something about the word exhilarated him. It seemed to speak of those faraway places that forever tugged at his young heart.

"What do you think about missionaries, Raymond?" one of the men inquired, a strange smile lurking around his mouth.

"Well, I think I might like to be one someday," the boy replied innocently.

"That's good, son. But you can't be a missionary unless you're born again."

"Born again? What do you mean by that?"

"Well, you see, we're all born once from our mothers. That's called being born of the flesh. But when we're born again, we're born of the Spirit of God."

Raymond stared at the man, trying to absorb his words.

Jim continued, "Do you know if you'll go to Heaven when you die, Raymond?"

"If I'm good and do the best I can, I think I will. Yes."

"No, you won't! That's not enough. You must be born again to go to Heaven."

A well-worn Bible suddenly appeared. The third chapter of the Book of John was opened, and the ancient story of Jesus' conversation with Nicodemus was read. This age-old message of eternal love was offered to Raymond Ross, just as it has been to millions of others in every land for nearly two thousand years.

For God so loved the world that He gave His only begotten Son that whosoever believeth on Him should not perish but have everlasting life.

The words lingered in the boy's mind as he raced home for lunch. He quickly ate, then went to his crowded bedroom. If I'm meant to be born twice, then I'd better do something about it, he reasoned. And so it was that he knelt alone beside his bed. "God, I want to be born again." His simple prayer was spoken almost silently.

When he returned to work in the afternoon, the subject of missionaries was raised once again.

"I'd like to be a missionary, I think." Raymond repeated his earlier statement.

"Well, I told you, you'll have to be born again first."

"But I am!"

With some effort, the story emerged. Jim was delighted.

"Look, Raymond, I'm to preach at the Derry Guild Hall next Sunday. Why don't you come along? The Bible says 'If you confess with your mouth the Lord Jesus and believe in your heart that God has raised Him from the dead you shall be saved.' You've believed. I can see that. But now you need to confess with your mouth to others what you've done."

The very thought of speaking out in a large crowd made Raymond feel slightly dizzy. Memories of past embarrassments haunted him. But he wanted more than anything else to do what was right. And so, when the day came around, he accompanied Jim and his wife to Derry on the bus.

After the sermon came the moment of confession. "Would anyone here care to stand up and give public testimony of their faith in Jesus Christ?"

Raymond's fingers tingled. His face flamed. He rose weakly to his feet, opened his mouth, and that was the end of it. He began to feel faint. Just as he had done during the music performance, he passed out.

After he regained consciousness and the horrifying crisis had passed, he concluded, *If I'm to be saved by confessing with my mouth, God is just going to have to find some other way of me doing it. That's the last time I'll ever try to speak in public again.*

A New Call and a New Voice

In the days to come, the boy thought long and hard about his "new birth." *There's not much point in trying to preach,* he reasoned, a wry smile twisting his mouth. *And I won't be doing much writing either. I guess the one thing I can do is pray.*

Painstakingly, he made a list. He was the only person who could have possibly read it, so illegible was his writing. But on it were the names of twenty-five young friends from Coleraine and the surrounding countryside. *The Bible says that with God, nothing's impossible,* he reasoned. *And the greatest miracle I can think of would be for my friends to be converted!*

Within six months, all twenty-five people on Raymond's list had made an individual decision to give their lives to Jesus Christ.

As months passed, new friendships were made. New bonds were formed in small prayer meetings and quiet conversations. Raymond was feeling a sense of gratitude to God for allowing him to be born again. He enjoyed listening to discussions about the Bible. About answered prayer. About the Christian way—a different way of living than he'd known before.

One Saturday he and a group of other believers prayed well into the night. During that meeting he felt a strong inner impression—an instruction regarding his participation in the church service he would attend the following day.

Next morning found Raymond at a small gathering. During an informal time of worship before the Lord's Supper was served, he again had the distinct feeling that he should stand and lead in prayer. On the one hand he was terrified at the prospect of such a thing. But on the other he sensed that God was directing him to do the impossible.

And so once again he sat, nervously twisting his hands, unhappily remembering the Derry Guild Hall disaster. At last the moment came. He stood up. He tried to speak. I'm going to faint again, he thought miserably.

But this time the experience was far different. Something unexpected was happening. A warm, burning sensation blazed in his throat. It moved upward into his mouth. It was almost fiery, and yet painless. He was speaking … or was he?

Electricity gripped the small service. Rapt eyes were on the young man's face. They all knew him, and yet this wasn't like him at all. The words he was speaking sounded foreign, unfamiliar. And he seemed so remarkably alive.

When the service concluded, talk was subdued. This was in no way a group with a Pentecostal tradition. They were unprepared for such an extraordinary manifestation of God's love. No one had any idea what to say.

But as for Raymond Ross, more than a passing miracle had happened to him. His halting speech was gone—forever. He was healed at the very moment the "fire" touched his mouth. And beyond the new freedom he felt in speaking, he was gripped with zeal.

He was filled with joy. He wanted to tell everyone he saw about the power of God.

He talked to friends. He talked to acquaintances. He approached people from the "better side of town" with the same good news that had transformed his own poverty marred life.

Before long he took to the streets of Coleraine and Portstewart. He preached. He pleaded. He poured forth the old-fashioned New Testament Gospel to anyone and everyone who could hear the sound of his voice.

Neighbours who had observed his childhood struggles shook their heads sadly. "Poor Raymond Ross ... he's a bit simple, isn't he?" Housewives clucked their condolences to one another. But a few people listened. And those who did heard a far different story.

The words the boy was saying were not the words of a simpleton. Far from it. There was a ring of truth. A sense of conviction. And a power that the small, fragile boy could have never found in his own strength.

"You mustn't stay in Northern Ireland," Lavina Ross had told her adopted son in many a conversation. "With all the unemployment, there's really nothing here for you, Raymond."

He had always vaguely understood that she was right. Ulster was home, yes. But never to explore the world? Never to see beyond the countryside that bordered the River Bann in endless green?

And now, as his thoughts became more and more focused upon spreading the message of Christian hope and salvation, her faith as words took on a new significance. He was too young to leave. He was too poor to travel. And yet, with his own brand of youthful courage, he concluded that it was time to move on.

Within a matter of months the decision was made. I'm going to London, Raymond promised himself as he ceaselessly walked along the familiar streets, lost in thought. I'll find some kind of school in London. He felt more certain with every footstep he took. I'll go to London and I'll train to be a preacher!

THREE

STRANGE FACES, EXCITING PLACES

From Liverpool the train whisked past row upon row of brick dwellings—three-chimneyed structures which hinted that poverty persisted behind their white-curtained windows. Walled-back gardens flourished in weeds. In the distance Raymond could see the urban expanse that was his destination—the London of 1952.

Throughout the night, trains had passed each other like explosions. A roar, a flash of light, then silence. Raymond's occasional focus upon a fleeting stranger's face had punctuated his light sleep. Now, with the dawn he was wide awake, almost bristling with excitement. A single, five-pound note wadded in his pants pocket wasn't much of a financial base. But in bold faith and a brave spirit he owned a fortune.

His feet touched London at Easton Station. Yesterday's sailing from Ulster to Liverpool seemed days past as he concentrated on his next course of action. *I'll walk around for a while and think things through. Then I'll find a place to spend the night.* This simple conclusion freed him from the weight of deliberation. He set his course along new and unfamiliar streets. And as he walked, his mind outpaced his feet.

By now Raymond Ross had learned that his legal name was Robert Barnett. His birth mother had placed her maiden name on his birth certificate.

"Your mother was killed in the London Blitz," Lavina Ross had informed him when he began to ask questions. As far as he was concerned Lavina had always been his true mother. She had loved him and cared for him with a devotion that seemed incredible, considering the size of her family. And yet he often wondered about his birth mother. Where exactly had she died in London? What would she have looked like? What kind of person was she? And what about his father?

In any case, it was Raymond Robert Barnett who had struck out on his own at sixteen years of age. He had made his way to London to gain the education he would need to become a preacher of the Gospel.

What's so unusual about doing a thing like that? the young man wondered as he recalled the anxious friends that had bid him farewell.

After a marathon of walking, he found himself a boarding house. Two pounds for room and board didn't leave him much for the rest of his life. But money wasn't a particularly interesting subject to young Ray. There were more important things to discover. Besides, he could always get a job.

A Link with the Methodists

Next day the walking began once more. Just about the time his feet began to ache, Ray found himself staring at a sign on a building: METHODIST CENTRAL HALL.

He walked in the door. Before he could catch his breath, he found himself speaking to Arthur Ross, the Secretary of Candidates for the entire Methodist denomination.

"I guess you're just the person I need to see, sir. I want to train for the ministry."

The dignified gentleman could do nothing but stare in disbelief at the thin, unimpressive boy. "The ministry?" It might have been amusing, but there was something very serious in Raymond's eyes. Mr. Ross made a call. He located Ronald Marshall, warden of the Bermondsey Settlement. This was a Methodist outreach ministry in one of London's worst slums. Could the mission house a young man?

Another call to the church's youth department located Raymond a job. He would work for the denominations book department. It was a familiar assignment for him—pick-up and delivery. But through it he quickly learned the intricacies of London's streets—streets he had longed to know.

A letter was sent to the Methodist church in Coleraine. "We have a young man here from your town ... Do you know anything about him? He wants to be trained for the ministry ... with your recommendation he can be approved as a 'preacher on trial.'"

Ray had only occasionally attended services with the Methodists in Coleraine. Just once had he told a Bible story to the children there. But the Reverend D. Hall Ludlow remembered. He kindly sent a letter to London: "Yes, we know Raymond. He has preached in our church."

And so it was that Raymond Barnett found his unique place among the Methodists in London. The Reverend Arthur Ross and his colleague Dr. Colin Roberts spent a surprising amount of time conversing with the young man. "You have a good mind, Raymond. Someday I think you really will be in the ministry."

Raymond listened. He watched. Beyond any teaching he would ever receive, he knew of God's supernatural intervention in his own impossible life. Yet now he was hearing different things, new teachings that seemed somehow to remove the miraculous from the subject of theology.

The words sounded the same on the surface. The terminology was, in essence, familiar. But the foundations seemed different. The virgin birth of Jesus was in question. The infallibility of the Bible was not a certainty. And in light of these and other equally shaky concepts, there seemed no place for the transcendent power of God that Ray had already witnessed first-hand.

And yet these people were kind to him. They were so caring for the poor. The work that was going on around him in the Bermondsey Settlement was godly work, righteous work.

Yes, it was bad theology—of that he was sure. He simply could not accept the weakened, impotent God that some of these theologians seemed to have devised. But the deeds were good deeds. *I believe*, Raymond told himself one day as he splashed through an autumn downpour, *that I will always have the mind of a conservative. My own life allows me no other choice. But as for my heart, I pray that it will be the heart of a liberal—reaching out to the poor, caring for the homeless, doing the things Jesus did when He was here on earth. Can't I be both?*

Questions Answered and a Dream Come True

The days with the Methodists drew to a close near Christmas in 1952. At seventeen, Raymond felt he should return to Ireland, at least for a while. There was no way he would ever be a Methodist minister. He realized that by now. But he gratefully said goodbye to his mentors. And he left London with mixed emotions. Certainly he would return, but at a different time and for a different reason.

During this period of time, a startling twist of relationships provided him with the name and identity of his birth father—a Coleraine acquaintance. Suddenly Ray understood childhood memories of a kind man named Bob Letson who had picked him up from school from time to time, a person who had occasionally stopped by for tea, just to say hello and to visit with the slow-speaking little boy. Ray felt a quiet love for the man and peace just in knowing a little more about his own history.

In all of this, a continuing zeal to serve God gave Ray a determination to press on in his efforts to study, to learn all he could possibly know about the Bible and its wonderful Author. Not long after his return from London, an evangelistic tour of Ulster by Dr. John Wesley White and his Irish bride provided him with the name of a school in a faraway land.

"Ray, you should think about attending the Full Gospel Bible Institute in Eston, Saskatchewan."

Canada! The very name of the place had stirred him as long as he could remember. Of course that's where he would go! It would certainly take some careful explaining to calm the friends and loved ones who had just welcomed him back to Coleraine. And it would take some doing to get there.

Hands in pockets, the young man smiled to himself as he took his favourite walk along the River Bann. As usual the logistics were seemingly insurmountable. But the idea was irresistible. "Ray Barnett," he almost laughed out loud with delight, "I think you'll be going to Canada. And I don't think it'll be long before you leave." His stride quickened as he made up his mind.

Fresh Beginnings in Calgary

Ray was right in his surmises on that walk along the River Bann. He did find his way to the Bible school in western Canada. And it didn't take too many years for him to do so. By 1957 he had completed his first year there and returned to Coleraine afterward. It had been a good year for him, but also a very difficult one. He had been homesick, and his difficulties in writing made it almost impossible for him to produce the many written reports for classes.

When a local church in Coleraine asked him to be their pastor temporarily until a permanent replacement could be found, he wondered if it wasn't God's will for him to stay in Ireland for good. But a man who heard him preach brought God's message to Ray. Hubert Nesbitt came to Ray after a service and told Ray that God wanted him to go back to school. To ensure this, God had directed Nesbitt to provide Ray with a one-way ticket back to Canada!

By the time 1961 rolled around, Ray was well settled into a whole new way of life. He graduated from Bible school where he had met a lovely classmate, Ruth Greaves.

They fell in love and married. Within a year they welcomed their firstborn son, Robert Ross Barnett, into the world. Meanwhile, Ray carried on evangelistic work across the prairie and mountain areas of Canada.

But on one particular day in July, Ray found himself troubled by an unknown worry. As he drove toward Calgary from High River, where he'd been holding evangelistic meetings, his eyes never focused on the towering Rocky Mountain peaks ahead of him or noticed the gleaming blue Alberta sky. As he drove, his mind was whirling with ideas.

What am I struggling with? Ray had asked himself that question again and again. His growing dilemma had made him irritable with the people around him. Impatience smouldered inside, sometimes burning through into his conversations.

He frequently thought back over the years. The early days in Coleraine. His rebirth. His healing. His time with the Methodists ... ah, yes, the Methodists.

They'd never approve of my evangelism. He smiled a little at the thought of Arthur Ross and Colin Roberts squirming through one of his salvation messages. But they sure had some good things to say. Things about reaching out to the world. Doing instead of just talking. Did today's journey to Calgary represent the solution to Ray's puzzle?

P. Lawson Travel Agency was a thriving, respected firm in Alberta. Ray was about to approach the president, Ken Lawson, with an inspiration from which he'd been unable to escape. He parked the car, rescued his somewhat crumpled coat from the backseat and rushed in the door.

After the necessary formalities and a welcome cup of hot coffee, the conversation really began. "What would you think," Ray had worded his question carefully during the morning drive, "of having a person, a person like myself, handling nothing but religious and missionary travel? I really believe I could bring a lot of business in here. And it would provide a valuable service to the church community."

The dialogue continued. Both Mr. Lawson and his colleague, John Powell, seemed intrigued. Why hadn't someone thought of doing this before? A respected minister with an interest in travel was the perfect candidate for such a job. But suddenly Powell said something that caused his potential employee a moment of near panic. "Why don't you write up a proposal, Ray? It's a great idea, all right. But I'd like to see it in writing."

"Dear God! Written reports nearly brought my education to an untimely end." Ray prayed desperately. "To this day I can't put my thoughts on paper to save my life. What now?"

Ken Lawson eyed Ray carefully. This is an unusual guy, Lawson thought to himself. One of those creative types, I guess. Finally he chuckled. "No, John. I'll tell you what. We'd better hire him now. If you make him write the thing up, I have a hunch he'll go across the street and get a job there." He motioned toward the shining bank of windows that housed the competition.

And so it was that Ray Barnett began his adventures in the travel business. Soon he was arranging tours. Booking flights. Guiding groups of pilgrims into the Holy Land. And during this time, he became acquainted with the activities of a group called Full Gospel Businessmen's Fellowship International.

Invited by several friends in the Northwest area, Ray attended a FGBMFI convention in Seattle during the 1962 World's Fair. He was housed, along with a number of others, at Seattle Pacific College and rode into the convention each day with a gentleman named John Peters. The man was president of a relief work known as World Neighbours.

"Most of our efforts are in Asia," Peters told Ray the first evening as the windshield wipers cleared away streams of unrelenting raindrops. While John Peters spoke about the commitment he had to the people of Asia, Ray felt a familiar excitement that had awakened within him so often before.

Ray was deeply impressed by all he heard. Now here's a man doing two things at once—helping people as well as spreading the Gospel, he thought. He's got the right idea.

Airlift to London

Not long after the Seattle convention had concluded, Ray and his family moved from rural Saskatchewan to Calgary, Alberta. His work with P. Lawson travel was flourishing. And by the time the Barnett family was settled, Ray was also putting together an ambitious new idea of his—an "Airlift to London." It would be a massive Full Gospel Businessmen's Convention in the U.K.

In late fall 1966, Ruth, Ray, and little Robbie arrived in London to see the dream become reality. While Ray worked on last-minute details at the convention headquarters, Robbie explored his father's favourite city with Ruth. Ray arrived in the hotel lobby to meet them one evening, only to discover the youngster in the fountain, fully clothed, delighting in his own brand of international adventure.

The results of the airlift were even more impressive than anyone had

like a Bill Gothard seminar

dared hope. Royal Albert Hall is said to seat more than ten thousand people. On the convention's final Saturday night, the Hall began to fill long before the meeting was to begin. It was estimated that another ten thousand people had crowded together outside, trying to catch the inspiring words that drifted from the packed auditorium.

Scores of men and women asked God to grant them a spiritual birth through Jesus Christ. Countless people made their way home through the London night possessing spiritual gifts they'd never hoped could be theirs. Gifts of love. Of wisdom and knowledge. Of physical and emotional healing. Of unknown languages that bypassed their human understanding.

A spark had been ignited within the United Kingdom. Teams of Christian evangelists were sent to Western Europe, Scotland, Wales and Northern Ireland. Soon the charismatic renewal would sweep the entire world with its fire. And when that time arrived, the kindling was already aflame in Britain and Western Europe because of the FGBMFI London Airlift.

"Well, how do you feel about your airlift brainstorm, now that everything's said and done?" his good friend Jerry Jensen asked him as they parted at Heathrow, each of them headed for home.

Ray's eyes seemed to focus on some faraway place. Then he replied, "Jerry, more than ten years ago I left Ireland for the last time. They thought I was crazy to go to Canada. Everyone begged me not to go, and I didn't know what to say to them. Finally I promised them that if I went, I'd do something for them that I could never do if I stayed in Ireland."

Jerry looked at him quietly for a moment. "So you've kept your promise?"

"Jerry, a lot of people had their lives changed forever this week. And when they go home, they'll have a miracle to report. I think I've kept my promise. I really think I have."

Stockholm and Growing Unrest

Less than a year later Ray was again at an international convention. This one was in Stockholm, Sweden, and he had worked hard with others to organize it. But this time his feelings about the event were very different. The London conference had excited him. He had been a part of something that would see lives changed all over the world. He had done something special for his countrymen in Northern Ireland. But now he wasn't so sure if convention planning was where he belonged ...

One morning instead of having breakfast with the rest of the staff and convention attendees, he went off by himself to do some thinking. At first he felt a sense of relief as he began his solitary walk. But it was only temporary. The troubled emotions that had washed over him in waves ever since his arrival in Stockholm were beginning to demand his attention. He needed to face up to something. But what was it?

Last year's London Airlift had been an amazing accomplishment. Everyone knew that. And along with others, Ray had been equally successful organizing this Swedish convention. Yes, all the people had arrived. Yes, evangelistic teams would soon be going out into Scandanavia and beyond, even behind the Iron Curtain. Yes, great spiritual tales of triumph were already being told. So why the dissatisfaction?

Ray had just celebrated another birthday. He was thirty years old now with two children—his first little daughter, Rheanne, had been born just five months before. But was this Christian organizational work supposed to be his future? It just didn't seem to fit. There had to be something different ahead of him.

"God, was I wrong to leave the ministry?" he asked silently as his feet carried him past autumn flowers that neatly decorated the Scandanavian avenues. They heralded another changing season, and life was passing too quickly. For a moment tears stung his eyes. *Did I misunderstand? I felt sure I was following Your will when I quit. But sometimes everything around me seems so meaningless. Why this emptiness?*

Ray made his way back to the Grand Hotel, to the control center for the convention. The office there never stopped buzzing with phone calls and questions. He'd made that room the center of his world for two weeks.

As he entered the suite, conversation between two workers seemed to end abruptly. They looked up at him with the slightly guilty look that said, "Oh ... we were just talking about you."

A brief exchange of words quickly revealed that Ray hadn't done something he'd been expected to do. "Too many loose ends, Ray." One of the men said as kindly as possible in the midst of his annoyance. "You need to get organized. Why don't you write out a schedule for yourself every morning? Make a list of things to do. Then follow it. That way the loose ends will be tied up."

Ray dismissed himself from the office as gracefully as he could. Within seconds he was walking again, faster and more deliberately than ever. Loose ends. Loose ends. What is my problem? It's always the same story. The job gets done. Everything gets done right. But people are upset with me from start to finish. I know I'm not lazy ... I never stop. And I know I'm not stupid. So what is it? I just don't seem to do things the way other people do them.

It would be nearly twenty more years before Ray would learn about or understand his specific learning disability. Until then, his exceptional gifts of intelligence, creativity, and intuition would be frequently overshadowed by discouraging limitations of skill and emotion. The fact that there might be a simple physiological explanation never crossed his mind.

So the earlier depression he had been feeling seemed to be compounded after his conversation with the disgruntled assistant. Ray's body surged with frustration and impatience. My mind's made up about one thing, anyway, he thought. I've done my best. Of that I am sure.

He remembered an earlier criticism made by a co-worker in an evangelistic organization. "Ray Barnett never reports anything in writing. How do we know what he's really doing?"

The well-known evangelist for whom they were both working had responded with a laugh. "Just leave Ray alone. He'll get the job done. He'll do more than he says he'll do. And he'll do it right." Ray felt a flush of warm comfort at the memory of those words. Within minutes he headed back to his hotel room, totally drained. Stretching out on the bed, he fell asleep.

One Woman's Problem

Later that day, Ray was back in the office again, surrounded once more by the familiar chaos of the convention. Questions came from all directions.

"I'm going with the team to Denmark. Where do I catch my bus?"

"Is it okay for me to sneak some New Testaments into Russia?"

"Do you know how much a dollar is worth in Finnish markkas?"

Then came a young journalist from Canada. "I'd like to go with your team of businessmen into Estonia. My grandmother is there, and it would give me a chance to visit her."

Somewhat preoccupied, Ray looked at the woman. She had already made it clear to him that she was not a Christian. He quickly considered the possibilities. *Maybe she'll find the Lord there if she goes.* "I don't see why not, Christa. Just get yourself a visa from the Soviet Embassy."

The next day the young newspaper reporter was back. "I think I need to talk to you, Ray. I've got a little problem."

Ray and Christa went to the hotel cafe. "So what's the problem, Christa?"

"Well, I didn't get my visa. They asked me if I had any relatives in Russia. I didn't know what to say on the application so I marked 'no.' And I think they knew it wasn't true. Anyway, how am I going to go to Estonia without a visa?"

Ray sighed as he considered the problem. A heavy weariness gripped him again. "Christa, I think you should go back to the Soviet Embassy. Tell them the truth. Admit that you were afraid—that you thought your grandmother might be sent to a labor camp or something. See what happens."

By nightfall, Christa came back to report that she had her visa. "Thanks, Ray! How did you know I'd get it if I went back?"

Ray shrugged and grinned. They continued to talk. He almost hated to admit it to himself, but he found it refreshing to converse with someone from outside the Christian world. As with others whom he'd met in the travel business, the young woman's perspective was startling. Through the drone of activity around the convention hive, she could see the many levels of human weakness. And she was quick to point them out.

When they parted that evening, Ray thoughtfully watched her go. There's a whole world out there that I know nothing about. I've spent my entire existence on the outside looking in. Sure, I'm always in the middle of something or other. But maybe I'm missing out on real life. Maybe ...

Next morning the teams left for their various destinations. A welcome lull ensued. During those quiet moments, Ray held his entire lifetime in his hands like a sphere. He examined it. He puzzled over it. He considered every conceivable alternative. It was clearly time for a new direction. But what would that direction be?

A Simple Question

A handful of days later Ray was bidding the Canadian journalist good-bye at the airport. He hadn't had even a moment since her return from Estonia to ask her about her trip.

"How was it? Did you see your grandmother?"

"Oh, yes. My grandmother was fine." Her thoughts seemed far away. She pushed a lock of dark blonde hair away from her eyes and looked at Ray.

"Grandmother was fine. But are you aware of the situation those Russian Christians are in?"

"Well, yes, a Finnish pastor was telling me something about it a few days ago. And of course everybody knows it's difficult."

"Ray, it's unbelievable. Those poor people risked a great deal taking me to an underground church meeting. They wept at the sight of people from the free world. It meant everything to them just to know that somebody cared."

Ray was stunned by the girl's intense response. It was completely unexpected, considering her own personal non-Christian philosophy. His amazed, silent expression prompted her to continue.

"They have absolutely nothing. They've lost it all—given it all up for their belief in God. Your friend Jerry Jensen gave one old man his ball-point pen. It was a treasure to the man. He burst into tears! Everyone you talked to has been beaten and harassed. And a lot of them have been imprisoned. Yet they're completely fearless.

"The day we left on the boat, there couldn't have been a more grim, military setting. Gunboats guarded the harbour. Everything around the dock said 'Danger!' And yet over a hundred people showed up to tell us good-bye. They all knew that their names would be recorded by the authorities just for being there. But there they were anyway.

"The last sound I heard as I left the shore of Russia was their singing fading across the water. A man told me they were singing a song called 'When We All Get to Heaven, What a Day of Rejoicing That Will Be.'"

It was a portrait of courage that Ray could grasp instinctively; it was almost as if he had been present. His own circumstances seemed suddenly insignificant at the thought of those valiant believers, radiantly smiling farewell to their free-world visitors.

"Ray, why don't you help them?"

They said good-bye. Her plane took off. The final details of his responsibilities had to be handled. The Stockholm convention was over, and Ray certainly didn't have all the answers he'd been seeking in the beautiful Swedish capital.

But in spite of everything, something revolutionary had happened to Ray. Once again there had been an instant recognition of God's clear direction. Once again the strong, inner voice of the Spirit had broken through. Once again a word of wisdom had been received.

In the midst of all the questions, a clear vision for reaching out to persecuted Christian believers had been given. The journalist had simply asked, "Why don't you help them?"

Ray Barnett had wordlessly answered, "Yes, I will."

And, before many more years had passed, help them he would.

FOUR

ROCKY BEGINNINGS

"Dear Friends in the West ... " was the way suffering Christians in the Eastern bloc countries often began their letters to caring brothers and sisters in the free world. So "Friends in the West" was the name everyone agreed on for the fledgling human-rights effort that officially began five years after Stockholm. And it was a good name, reflecting the spirit of the work.

Ray began to establish contacts. He investigated ways of reaching out to believers who had been deprived of their freedom. Ruth worked night and day, caring for the children, managing the household, and doing all the necessary paperwork for the ministry. She typed letters, stuffed and sealed envelopes. The living room became headquarters for the effort.

"Ruth, I hate to be gone so much ... " Ray always felt torn when it came time to leave the family again. He missed them all, and yet the work simply could not be done without travel.

"Well, Raymond, I think we made that decision years ago—you go when you have to go. I'll stay home and take care of things here. That's just the way it has to be."

So Friends in the West was born with the intent to help those in need.

"Prayer is the point," Ray would intensely explain to people, his eyes glowing with enthusiasm. "Real, sincere prayer for struggling Christians behind the Iron Curtain can change the course of history! We'll be their friends—their prayer partners. That's where we'll start. Then we'll see what happens!"

Ray started raising money to make trips into Communist bloc countries to contact those who needed the friendship and prayers of Christians in the West. One of his first missions concerned some believers in Czechoslovakia. In 1972 he visited the ancient city of Prague.

A New Task for Friends in the West

Colourful Czech and Soviet banners rustled in the slight breeze as Ray made his way across Wenceslas Square. Cobbled roads roared uncomfortably with the passing of modern cars. And delicate church spires rose against the clear sky above the bustling streets.

Ray glanced at the statue of the "Good King" that towered over the famous square. Prague's a lovely old place, he thought to himself. But as he restlessly waited to cross at a streetlight, he wondered, what next? What should I do now?

He had flown into Prague the day before. On behalf of Friends in the West, he was there to continue efforts to aid imprisoned Czech Christians. Such journeys, dangerous though they often were, had become vital to the work.

But a nagging thought was keeping step with him as he walked. He reviewed the preceding days. Had God told him to do something? Was he subtly evading His directions? Should he really be somewhere else?

His trip from North America had been made in several stages. The first leg had taken him from Seattle to Denver to fulfil a speaking engagement. On that particular journey he had been reading, as usual, when the flight attendant arrived to take drink orders.

"Coffee, please ... " he had replied without thinking. As he looked up at the young woman he noticed a heavy, silver-tone bracelet at her wrist. It appeared to have a name inscribed on it.

"Your coffee, sir." When she interrupted him again, his eyes were drawn once more to the strange-looking bangle.

"Thanks ... yes, cream, too. Thank you. Can you tell me about your bracelet? It's unusual, isn't it?"

"Oh, well yes. It's a P.O.W. bracelet. The man whose name is on it is in a Vietnamese prison camp. The idea is to wear it until he's released."

Ray had stared out the oval aircraft window, unconsciously drinking his coffee. He watched streams of mist streak behind the wing as the nucleus of an idea formed in his mind. Prisoners. Prisoners of war. Bracelets.

How many persecuted Christians were imprisoned around the world? He couldn't begin to guess. The threadbare phrase "spiritual battle" occurred to him. It may be a spiritual battle, he thought, but some of the captives are in real prisons with real guards. And there must be thousands of them.

He recalled a relevant Scripture verse: "Remember those who are in prison, as though you were in prison with them" (Hebrews 13:3, GNB). What better way to be chained to another person than to wear a bracelet bearing his name?

What if Friends in the West made Prisoner-for-Christ bracelets to remind people to pray? To bind them to someone who's suffering?

The flight attendant reappeared. Ray automatically lowered the tray in front of his seat. His dinner was handed to him, and he began to unwrap the plastic-covered food. But his mind was still on the bracelets. Do something about it, Ray. A familiar flutter, an inner stirring had touched him. And that was all.

Messages in Music

All the distraction of changing planes, retrieving luggage and passing customs eclipsed Ray's attention after those still, small thoughts first hit him. But now that he had finally arrived at his Eastern European destination, their whispered message became more persistent. As he walked past marketplaces and busy shops, a sense of unease prevailed.

Music drifted from some invisible radio inside a store. All at once the song's lyric broke into his awareness: "Put your hand in the hand of the Man who stilled the waters. Put your hand in the hand of the Man who calmed the sea." In Prague? he thought with amazement. In English? He smiled broadly at the marvel—a Christian song filling the streets of a Communist city.

He was suddenly, joyfully aware of a welcome Presence. And he made an abrupt decision. If I'm going to put my hand in His, I'd better be on my way to where He's calling me to go. I've got to fly to London—as soon as I possibly can!

With that, Ray determined that he would complete his mission in record time. He worked relentlessly. And the instant he felt sure he'd accomplished all he could, he headed for the airport with but one thought in his mind: get the bracelets made.

He did just that. Soon the very first group of bracelets was manufactured. They were inscribed with the strange-sounding names of unknown heroes—names like RODOSLAVOV. RYTIKOV. SKRIPNIKOVA. KRIUKCHOV.

The prayer bracelets were an immediate success. Hundreds of people requested them. And in the wearing, thousands of lives were touched. As they explained the purpose of their bracelets, Christians found new opportunities to share their faith with others. Well-fed, fast-paced believers in the West were taking the time to pause and pray for their hungry and hurting counterparts across the sea. Even little children were treasuring bracelets of their own, writing carefully printed letters that promised sweet, simple prayers.

The bracelets were worn by celebrities—people like Pat Boone, and Dean Jones. They were talked about on television. They were introduced through the media. They were taken to the four corners of the world. And, before long, the prayers they generated clearly began to take effect. News triumphantly leaked out through secret channels:

GENNADII KRIUKCHOV: out of prison and in deep hiding.
PAVEL RYTIKOV: released from prison.
AIDA SKRIPNIKOVA: out of prison—again—but still witnessing for Christ!

Ray could smile to himself as he reviewed each prisoner's case. Like silent music, the eloquent words of the prophet Isaiah floated through his mind: "The Lord has ... sent me to bind up the broken-hearted ... to proclaim liberty to the captives, and the opening of the prison to those who are bound" (61:1).

But glancing at the scattered papers on his desk, he sighed and shook his head. There are so many others still in bondage! By that time, Friends in the West was in direct contact with the families of dozens of imprisoned Christians. Letters smuggled out of the Soviet Union by courageous underground couriers were revealing horrifying tales of violent arrests, brutal beatings, and nightmarish oppression.

One particular name was being repeated more and more frequently. The secretary of the Council of Baptist Churches in Kiev had been arrested for the first time in 1966 and had been taken into custody repeatedly since. He had been carried away secretly, hidden from his relatives. He was accused of infringing the laws relating to religious worship, of shirking socially useful work and of vagrancy.

I've got to get a bracelet out with his name on it. In fact, I'm going to take care of it right now. Ray painstakingly printed the name, intently comparing it to a printed document to make sure he had it right. He picked up the phone and dialled.

"Yes, hello, this is Ray Barnett at Friends in the West. I want to order some more bracelets ... Yes. Let's start with a thousand. This is a name we haven't ordered before. The name is GEORGI VINS. Let me spell it for you."

Betrayed by Frailty

That same year of 1972, which saw so many victories and clear leadings from God, however, also brought with it Ray's greatest test of faith so far.

One day as he arrived at the small, newly established office of Friends in the West, another north western rainstorm was blowing in from the sea, but Ray's heart was at peace. Life had not always been easy over the past years, but his list of valuable underground contacts had grown steadily. He had relentlessly gathered the names and information necessary to aid persecuted Christian believers. And above all else, his heart was in what he was doing.

He jumped out of the car at the post office, grabbed the mail out of the Friends in the West mailbox and drove on. When he arrived at the little office, he ripped open a couple of letters expectantly. Then he quickly scanned the third communication.

What he read paralyzed him with horror. A quick note from a friend was attached:

Dear Ray,

This arrived at my home this morning. I've also learned that the individual who sent it has fraudulently used my name to gain further credit information. Were you aware that this letter had been sent?

A quick survey of the attached document caused Ray to collapse into a chair, sickened with shock. It was, quite simply, a credit report on Ray Barnett. It listed every black mark that had ever appeared on his record, along with a number of current accounts. The text strongly implied that Ray had used money dishonestly, that he was not to be trusted, and that his ministry should not be supported.

The letter bore no signature, but Ray guessed from whom it had come. Yet the important thing was not who had done this, but what was to be done now. Rain beat against the windows outside. Inside, Ray's heart beat as if it would burst out of his chest. How many people have seen this thing? The question gnawed at his insides. To whom was it sent? He stared at the dripping windows, immobilized by the magnitude of the malicious letter.

Ray knew very well how the whole matter had come about. Five years before, he had broken away from P. Lawson Travel and started his own travel agency. For a number of reasons the venture had not done well. Into the effort Ray had carried his chronic lack of organization, his poor grasp of numbers, and his inability to put things into writing. All these factors had contributed to a marked lack of success.

External circumstances had been equally devastating. An airline had not come through with an offer to underwrite the business. A trusted employee had gravely misused authority in handling funds. The list of contributing factors went on and on.

If I had declared bankruptcy in the first place, this never would have happened, Ray kicked himself mentally. *The attorneys told me to take that route. Why did I make it such a matter of conscience? I never did get everybody paid back. And now this ...*

All the furor over the Calgary travel agency had brought about investigations by the Royal Canadian Mounted Police. And because American nonprofit organizations were involved in the international religious tours he was booking, further inquiries had been made by the United States Internal Revenue Service. Naturally curious local journalists had continued the quest.

After all was said and done, not one trace of evidence was ever found to indicate any criminal or unethical activity on Ray's part. No one would deny, least of all himself, that he could have done business more efficiently. If he'd even begun to understand his disabilities at the time, he would have hired people to do the tasks that he found most difficult. And he could have used better judgment when it came to promptly setting the record straight and protecting his name.

But now all that was history. This one vicious letter might ruin his future ministry once and for all. In the hours that followed the initial outrage, one question cut into Ray like a knife: *Why didn't I do something about this sooner? I spin my wheels. I lose myself completely in whatever it is I'm doing. And suddenly months have passed. Next thing I know years have gone by. And still I haven't handled things.* For hours he walked the wet city streets, chastising himself.

A Time for Deciding

Subsequent days brought even more devastating news. The letter had apparently been sent to everyone on the Friends in the West mailing list. It had also been addressed to Christian leaders, to people who could, with a public word, destroy everything Ray had ever hoped to accomplish.

After the letter had begun to circulate, the Barnetts noticed a gradual change in the behaviour of certain friends. They detected a cooling from some, a subtle avoidance from others. Few people actually addressed the situation; they just quietly drifted away.

Sometimes Ray watched his three children playing: Rob, Rheanne and now Rhonda, a blue-eyed daughter of two who toddled around behind her brother and sister. They were carefree—oblivious to their father's anguish. And yet their futures might be forever marred by it. The thought sickened Ray.

Personal rejection was nothing new to him. He had experienced it in varying degrees ever since his early, slow-speaking days in the Coleraine school yard. But now his family was hurt. Now his friends were disappointed. Now the lives of those faraway people he'd hoped to help were affected.

"Go after the person who did this!" Ray was advised by those who knew the whole story. "Get that person into court and let the truth be known. You've got to act!"

But Ray was emotionally unable to take such a step. Instead, he became obsessively fixed on questions of "Why?" and "How?" He endlessly tried to unravel knots of illogical explanations. And worst of all, he privately and ceaselessly blamed himself for the entire tragedy.

Within weeks, a trip behind the Iron Curtain became necessary. Weary with pain, weak with fatigue, Ray Barnett boarded a London-bound jet. He listlessly watched the wings of the aircraft cut through the last wispy clouds and burst into the blue sky beyond. He sighed a quiet prayer. "God, I'm like a man hanging onto a ledge by the very tips of my fingers. Don't let me fall, Lord. Please don't let me fall."

In his next thought, he made a sudden decision. *I think I should take a quick trip to Ireland before I get involved in anything else. Going back there just might help me sort everything out. Yes. I'm going to fly to Belfast tomorrow morning. That's what I'm going to do.*

FIVE

SIGNS AND WONDERS FROM GOD

Ray sat motionless on the wooden bench, facing the glistening north Atlantic waters. His arms were crossed, his legs thrust out in front of him. His face would have been unreadable to a passerby, reflecting none of the concern that weighed on his mind. Only the burning intensity of his eyes exposed his sadness.

As if it were a mother's hand reaching out in comfort, the constant Irish wind pushed his hair back from his forehead. Donegal Peninsula was clearly visible that day across the white capped waters. The sky was clear, but a distant bank of clouds on the horizon promised mist by evening.

Despite his burdened spirit, Ray was calmed by Portstewart's familiar surroundings. He had begun his life there, and no matter how circumstances spun and swirled around him, this particular place in the world seemed to remain forever unchanged. That awareness had quieted his spirit, just as an earlier walk along the sweeping beach had relaxed his body.

Now, like a child searching for seashells, he was silently sifting through his lifetime. As always, it seemed to him there was too much sand. Too little of value. Thoughts that had first tormented him in Stockholm came more gently now. Had he made the right move in leaving the evangelistic ministry? A procession of other long-past decisions waited in line for his appraisal. And, although his mood was placid, he felt he had no absolute answers regarding any course he'd ever taken.

Treasured supernatural wonders had faded into distant shadows. Only dimly could he see the splendour of the miracles that had confirmed God's hand upon his early years. Far clearer was the turmoil and travail that seemed to follow him wherever he went.

What about his present direction? Until recently he'd firmly believed that his desire to assist the persecuted church was a God-given vision. But the malicious letter had even made him question that reality. "Lord, what am I supposed to be doing with my life? Have I gotten completely off track? Am I headed in the wrong direction?" There was no great emotion in his unspoken prayer. Only a sense of resignation remained as he poured out his plight to God.

"My existence has been strange and unexplainable since the day I was born," he thought. "I should never have survived in the first place. I never knew my birth mother. I barely knew my father. I couldn't accomplish anything at school. I couldn't even speak until You healed me.

"There have been so many choices. Who to marry. Where to live. What to do. First it was evangelism. Then FGBMFI. Then the travel business. Then the persecuted church. And there has always been uncertainty. There's always been something unsettled. I'm really not sure about anything anymore, Lord, except that I can't give up.

"So here I am again, Lord, back at Portstewart. Back where it all started. And my request is simple. If I'm on the right track with my life, I'd like to hear from You today."

Going Home

With that Ray rose to his feet, located his rented car and began to drive. He had made no clear plans for the remainder of the afternoon, but a sudden impulse put him on the road to Derry.

"I think I'll see if I can find the house where my mother was supposed to have lived."

He'd known for years that an old residence at Culmore Point, just a breath from the border of the Irish Republic, had been his birth mother's home. Ever intrigued by her and her absence from his life, he had always intended to pay the place a visit. What better day to do it?

The road wound along tree-lined waters. Culmore Point marked the end of the River Foyle and the beginning of a tranquil, natural harbour. As he drove on, a sense of wonder stirred him. Even before Portstewart, his life had really begun right here.

At last he arrived at the house. It was unmistakably the right place. He'd heard enough about it to recognize it at first glance. Hundreds of years old, it was a miniature castle, guarding the entrance to the river. A grim reminder of ancient warriors and long forgotten battles, it had a curious mystique that fascinated Ray. A spontaneous smile tugged at his mouth.

He parked the car and began to explore the outside of the structure. Gulls cried out. Ripples quietly lapped against the shoreline. What a strange and unique place it was, so silent and empty. Tenaciously planted at the edge of the water, it had weathered more storms and tempests than could ever be counted.

Narrow, boarded-up slits in the stone walls provided the only windows. He tried to peek through, to catch a glimpse of the interior, but all he saw was darkness. "Maybe I can see through on the other side," he thought, making his way across the stone walkway that led toward the water's edge.

Suddenly, as if out of nowhere, a grizzled old fisherman appeared, his back to the bay. He looked at Ray with clear blue eyes. "What are you doing here?" his steady gaze seemed to ask.

Ray smiled at the salty-looking character. "This is an interesting old place."

"Yes, it is. It's owned by the London Irish Society. But they aren't taking very good care of it."

"Do you know anything about the people who lived in it? My mother grew up here but I never knew her. Did you ever hear of the Barnetts?"

The old man's blue eyes studied Ray carefully before he replied. Then he grinned. "Oh, yes. Your mother did grow up here. And you had a sister, too. She was adopted by a family named Wells before World War II. The man who adopted her worked on a dredger. Your sister's name was Iris, but her new family changed it. It's Catherine now, I think."

Ray began to frantically scribble notes in the little book he always carried with him. The fisherman continued his astounding report. "Your mother is still living. She's in New York City. I can give you her address." The information was recorded.

"The rest of the family lives in New Zealand. That's about all I can tell you."

Ray stared at the fisherman, his face radiant with wonder. Who was he? How could he have so many specific facts stored in his mind? How had he arrived from nowhere with such uncanny timing? In a matter of seconds the two of them would have missed each other forever.

At a loss for words, Ray could only say, "Thank you ... thank you very much. I really appreciate your help."

The old man nodded, touched his weather-beaten cap and walked away, fishing gear in hand.

Many Connections

As Ray delved into the story, it became evident that every word the fisherman had spoken was true. Ray carefully tracked down each lead. By the time a handful of seasons had come and gone, he had found his sister. Within a few years he was also in touch with his birth mother. Soon bridges were lovingly being built between the two women and the adopted Ross boy who had grown up in Coleraine.

The impossibility of all that would have been dramatic enough. But burned into Ray's mind was another miracle. "Lord, if I'm on the right track with my life, I want to hear from You today." That had been his simple prayer, offered up to Heaven from the Portstewart bench.

The answer hadn't come from behind the Iron Curtain. The response had made no mention of persecuted Russian Christians or of Soviet oppression. Instead, the message had been personally directed to his heart. God's sudden, split-second intervention had proved, beyond question, that He had been walking beside Ray Barnett all along.

The Father Himself would sift the years—past, present and future. Through the screen of eternity He alone could shake away the sands of futility. Of frustration. Of malicious letters and loose ends. With His skilful eye, only He could sort out the shimmering shells. The shining gemstones.

The treasures of a lifetime.

And what about the curious old fisherman? Ray's inquiries quickly revealed that no one living around Culmore Point had any idea who the wind-burned man with all the answers might have been. As far as anybody in the tiny community could recall, he had never been there before. No one had ever noticed him fishing in those waters. And to this day, he has never returned again.

But angel or common passerby, he had given Ray Barnett the comfort and assurance that he needed from God. Ray could go on with life, knowing that his goals were the right ones and that God was with him in his work. He returned home and went about the business of patching up his affairs after the disastrous negative publicity.

A well-trusted co-worker was given responsibility for handling funds. An accountant was hired to monitor the books on a regular basis. Financial statements, prepared by the accountant, began to be published annually and remain so to this day. It will never happen again, Ray would remind himself when painful memories jarred him. He knew his limitations all too well, and he determined that the mistakes of the past simply would not be repeated.

The Work Goes On

The tasks of Friends in the West continued unrelentingly, and once Ray got beyond this early crisis, his efforts began to bear much fruit. One day in 1975 he found himself in a beautiful but very dangerous situation. He was in Mozambique, watching the African sunlight play on the waters of the Indian Ocean. From his hotel window he could see the beach and the distant shoreline of Madagascar. But the peacefulness of the scene hinted nothing of the grave danger surrounding him.

Getting past the guards will be the trick, he reminded himself as he hurriedly dressed, tucking a small camera into his left sock. *But I did get into the country yesterday with the border closed! Nothing's impossible.*

For a moment he recalled his encounter at the rigidly protected border crossing. The day before he had driven across Swaziland. As Mozambique grew near, the traffic thinned dramatically. No cars or trucks were to be seen. Apparently no one else was going to "the Switzerland of Africa" that afternoon.

He abruptly reached the border. There Ray had faced a sober official. He'd spread out every piece of documentation in his possession while cheerfully carrying on a meaningless, one-sided conversation with the man. His passport had been presented, of course. Also his Canadian driver's license. He'd volunteered an odd assortment of personal identification and whatever else filled his bulging wallet. And he'd waited.

The somewhat puzzled government officer had examined the array of materials uncertainly. Just weeks before, Communist Frelimo rebels had finally overthrown the four-hundred-year-old Portuguese government of Mozambique. The border had remained closed, but the rules regarding visitors weren't particularly clear. And there was something about this North American tourist that seemed harmless enough. Why not let him in?

And so it was that Ray Barnett had entered the country. The roadways had been empty. The place was strangely silent. He had made his way to Maputo, a lovely city of tree-lined streets. After discreetly meeting with some contacts and checking into an all-too-deserted hotel, he had taken a moonlit walk on the beach and formulated his strategy.

Ray smiled a bit ironically at the sight of his lavish ocean view. *I could never have afforded to stay in such a luxury hotel three months ago,* he thought. *What a beautiful place!* This was obviously quite an elegant spot before the revolution. Now the rates were more than reasonable. Since the Frelimo takeover, tourists were as rare as capitalist slogans.

Finally dressed and ready to go to Maputo prison, Ray stood at the window a moment longer. He systematically reviewed the circumstances in his mind.

The Risks of Being a Missionary

Christian missionaries had been imprisoned at the time of the Frelimo takeover. One of them was a black man from Rhodesia (now Zimbabwe) who stood little chance of release because of his national background. They were all being held in a dangerous prison with a reputation for torture and brutality.

To Ray Barnett's way of thinking, the best hope for Salu Daka Ndebele, the jailed Rhodesian, was to broadly publicize his plight. A photograph of him in his prison cell distributed to the international wire services would accomplish that very nicely. Then, once Salu's situation was made known to the world, diplomatic steps could be taken with the new government.

If I'm caught with the camera, that'll be the end of it. Ray glanced at a mirror as he walked toward the door, smiling wryly at his reflection. *Well, I certainly don't look the part of a daredevil. Nondescript, that's the word. And I need to lose at least ten pounds.* Ray's inconspicuous appearance had protected him many times in the past. Perhaps the same would be true today.

When he arrived at the prison, he faced the possibilities calmly. As was often the case in such life-threatening circumstances, he felt a warm assurance. No guarantees of course, but somehow he sensed that his mission would be accomplished.

A line had formed outside the prison walls as the friends and relatives of those inside waited to be searched. One by one they lifted their arms and submitted to a rough frisking by unsmiling authorities. Ray anticipated his turn. Would they discover the camera in his sock?

Expert hands slapped him aggressively. He breathed a wordless prayer. His lower legs remained untouched, and the guard motioned him on. He stepped toward the next checkpoint, camera intact.

As he signed an official registry, the second group of guards wordlessly studied him. Their icy stares were meant to intimidate him. They retained Ray's passport. "You have just relinquished your freedom," they proudly seemed to say. "Keep the rules or you'll lose it forever."

Ray's eyes quickly assessed his surroundings. Although the exterior of Maputo prison was cold and unappealing, the courtyard was pleasant with shady trees and lush shrubbery. There was no point speculating what the facility was like on the inside. Maputo prison's record of violence was common knowledge. And somewhere between those walls was Salu, a young man whose life was gravely at risk.

Ray easily located the American missionaries who were imprisoned there: Don Milam, Armand Doll, and Hugh Friberg. It was visiting day for them, so they were able to converse in the outdoor visitation area. They spoke softly to Ray about their life there. Although they, too, were in jeopardy, their American passports and visibility carried a promise of eventual release. Not so for Salu.

"Where is he?" Ray had carefully examined the crowd for listeners before asking the question. One of the American missionaries directed his sight toward a row of cell-block windows across the yard. Within seconds Ray casually found his way there.

He glanced around quickly. No one seemed to have noticed his short walk away from the visiting grounds. The American missionaries had turned and looked the other way. Salu's window was just a little high for Ray to see through. He grasped the bars and hoisted himself up.

Hope in a Dark Cell

"Salu! Salu!" His voice broke through the silence within the walls. There was an immediate stirring inside the cell. When his vision adapted to the dimness, Ray could see the gleam of startled eyes.

"Who are you?"

"Walk over here. I've come to visit." Salu was astonished to see a smiling white face at the window.

"How can you be smiling! If the guards catch you, you won't smile anymore!"

Ray quickly removed the camera from his sock. The snap of its shutter seemed to resound like thunder. After taking a couple of shots he deftly returned it to its hiding place.

"How did you get a camera in here? They'll keep you locked up for the rest of your life if they find you with that."

"Salu, my name is Ray Barnett. I have a human-rights organization called Friends in the West. We heard about your situation, and I came here to help you. I'm going to put your picture in the paper all over the world. We're going to have prayer bracelets made with your name on them. Thousands of people will be praying for your release."

The young Rhodesian had been working with a group called Youth With A Mission before his incarceration. He believed wholeheartedly in prayer. But Salu was stunned. He was so sensitive to the danger of the situation, he could hardly grasp the hope and importance of what Ray was telling him.

"Ray, thank you for coming, but you'd better get out of here. Go back and mingle with the others. I may be executed. But there's no reason for you to be."

"Salu, you won't be executed. And I will never forget you until you are out of here. I will not forget you."

With that, Ray returned to the courtyard. Unexplainably, no one had seen him leave and no one seemed to notice his return. Within minutes he was out of the prison, his passport and exposed film in hand.

Within hours he was safely out of Mozambique, never to return. Within weeks the picture of Salu Daka Ndebele was published in the international press.

Months passed. Worldwide, surging tides of political uprising and terrorism seemed to swell on a daily basis. Human-rights violations exploded like breakers, relentlessly eroding the boundaries of freedom.

During those critical days, Ray Barnett sadly watched Idi Amin's rise to power in Uganda. He absorbed with a sense of despair the accelerating tension in the Middle East. As always he personally struggled along with the innocently oppressed behind the Iron Curtain. He never failed to explore his own usefulness in each crisis. He was never idle. His thoughts were never still.

But in the back of Ray's mind, there remained an awareness of a young man in prison. Just as he promised, Ray Barnett never forgot about Salu. *There's nothing I can do today,* he reminded himself a thousand times when impatience burned within him. *I'll just have to wait until the right time comes.*

Meanwhile, another name in another part of the world continued to repeat itself in Ray's mind. And in case memory didn't serve him well, the prayer bracelet he wore on his wrist would not allow him to forget.

"GEORGI VINS," it read. And when Ray prayed for the man, he wondered, *what can I possibly do to help him? The Bible says "Watch and pray." Well, I am praying. But I'm watching for a way to get Georgi Vins out of labor camp.*

SIX

FAITH AT WORK IN WASHINGTON

Summer had thrown a steaming, humid cloak around the city of Washington, D.C., that day in 1976. Along streets that swarmed with well-heeled government workers, faces were beaded with perspiration. Nevertheless, ceaseless activity prevailed. Above it all the United States Capitol Building gleamed in sun-burnished majesty, a familiar monument to freedom and democracy.

Deep within the Capitol walls, Ray Barnett sat transfixed by the proceedings. John Buchanan, a member of the House of Representatives from the state of Alabama, was speaking.

"In May, thirteen countries took part in a worldwide demonstration with the presentation of petitions totalling more than 600,000 names to Soviet Embassies, requesting the government to release Georgi Vins from prison ...

"I quote from Article 124 of the Soviet Union's Constitution: 'No one is forced to be a believer or an atheist, to observe religious rites or not to do so.' But in actual practice evangelism is prohibited; all churches must be registered and approved by the government; pastors are appointed by state committees; informers are reported to be in each congregation; pastors have been accused by their followers of betraying their own people to the authorities ...

"And as for Georgi Vins, unless some action is taken on his behalf, he will surely die in a hard labor camp in Siberia."

The setting was The United States House of Representatives Committee on International Relations. The subject was "Religious Repression in the Soviet Union: Dissident Baptist Pastor Georgi Vins." The hearing was a necessary step in passing through the U.S. Congress a resolution renouncing the Soviet Union. And the man who had initiated the entire undertaking was an Irish-Canadian named Ray Barnett.

As he sat listening to the testimony of the witnesses Friends in the West had assembled, he thought back across the months before. An unexpected expedition into international politics had led him into that place of influence. It amazed him somewhat just to be sitting there.

U.N. Contacts

For years Friends in the West had been receiving letters from oppressed Soviet people pleading for justice. Frequently these letters were addressed to the Secretary General of the United Nations. In a desperate attempt to help, Ray had made his way into United Nations headquarters in New York City.

The bureaucracy of the place had sent him from office to office. After several visits, he'd received virtually no help from anyone. At last he was introduced to the U.S. State Department's Senior Adviser for Human Rights. The man had been assigned to the United Nations in that official capacity for two years. His name was Guy Wiggins.

When Ray walked into his office the two men shook hands warmly. After the usual introductory formalities, Ray began to describe his organization. He tried to express his personal desire to aid persecuted believers.

A born again Christian, Wiggins had thought to himself. I've never had anything to do with these people before. This should be interesting. "I can tell you one thing, Ray," Guy Wiggins laughed with a note of cynicism in his voice. "If you think the United Nations is going to be of any use to you, forget it. This place is a dead end when it comes to human rights in the U.S.S.R—the Soviets have too much power."

Ray sized up Guy Wiggins without speaking. There was a wisdom about the man that came through as he spoke. He had been with the State Department for eighteen years. Not only did his career experience have to do with human rights, but he was equally well-versed in matters of commerce and economy. A clear-eyed pragmatist, he knew exactly what he was talking about.

"If you want my opinion," Wiggins went on to say, "you need to work through the United States legislative process, not through the U.N."

Ray laughed, "I'm not exactly an expert in the United States political system. But I can appreciate what you're saying—if the American government were to officially condemn Soviet human rights violations ..."

"A Congressional Resolution," Guy interrupted. "That's what needs to be made. It would put the entire nation on public record against Soviet religious repression."

Ray responded instantly and instinctively, nodding in affirmation. "That's what we'll do, then." His voice carried a certain authority and confidence that impressed Wiggins. "I have all the facts and contacts. You know the system. Too bad you're already working here!"

He may be inexperienced in the political arena, but there's something about this man that makes me believe in him, Wiggins thought. Besides I like his sense of humor. "I'll tell you what, Ray. I'm planning to retire in a couple of months. Why don't we talk about this again then? I have an idea we could get a lot accomplished if we worked together."

Fruitful Alliance

Within a few months the alliance was formed. The diplomatic doors were opened. The appropriate letters were written, making friendly but necessary overtures. Guy Wiggins expertly saw that one influential political office was put in contact with another. As his activity increased, so did the ground swell of support that accompanied this humanrights endeavor.

Meanwhile, Ray sought out experts whose observations would lend credibility to the project. He talked to those who knew, firsthand, how desperate the Christians' plight in the U.S.S.R really was. He set his best couriers to the task, at times working in secret and at great risk. Thanks to them, the required facts would be brought forth at the proper time.

In the midst of all this, one man emerged from the U.S. legislative system who would also become invaluable to the effort. He was the Honorable John H. Buchanan, Jr. A former Baptist minister himself, his concern for the religious rights of Christians behind the Iron Curtain led him to new levels of commitment. Like Guy Wiggins and Ray Barnett, this Alabama statesman worked tirelessly, leaving nothing to chance.

Buchanan eventually introduced House Concurrent Resolution 726. It received almost immediate support from both parties in the House of Representatives. It called for hearings of the House Committee on International Relations. Friends in the West and Ray Barnett would have to bring together the necessary witnesses for the hearings.

Ray wrote to a Norwegian contact, "Can you locate for us a Baptist pastor who has recently been expelled from the U.S.S.R. (or left for reasons of persecution) within approximately the last two years?"

The response came. The Reverend Janis Smits entered the scene, along with the Reverend David Klassen, both Russian Baptist pastors recently exiled and living in West Germany. Other witnesses would include Dr. Bohdan R. Bociurkiw, a professor at Carleton University in Ottawa, Canada; Dr. John Dunlop, a professor in the German Russian Department at Oberlin College in Ohio; Dr. Lev Dobriansky, professor in the Department of Economics at Georgetown University; and George Dobczansky, research director of Human Rights Research, Inc., in Washington, D.C.

God's Resources

The House hearings were scheduled for June 24 and 30, 1976. Just days before the proceedings, Ray discovered there wasn't enough money in the Friends in the West bank account to fly all the witnesses to Washington. Worse yet, Ray was hospitalized, recuperating from major surgery.

The man was frustrated beyond words. As the IV solution dripped into his arm, hours passed with unrelenting speed. His emergency operation had not been planned. It couldn't have happened at a worse time. The entire American political system was on an irreversible course, and Ray would be largely responsible for the outcome. Yet there he lay, immobilized, weak and worried.

At the last possible second and against his doctor's orders, he checked himself out of the hospital. Dizzy and clammy with sweat, he caught a plane. He gripped the armrest for support as the eastbound jet took off. *God, where and how am I going to locate enough airfare to get Janis Smits to Washington? I'm so sick I can't think straight. But we've got to get this thing done! I need Your help, Lord.*

As the aircraft cut through the failing daylight, an idea began to dawn in Ray's mind. He suddenly recalled a pastor who had once offered to help Friends in the West if an urgent need arose. What could be more urgent than this?

Within an hour Janis Smits would be arriving at Frankfurt airport, expecting to find his prepaid ticket to Washington awaiting him. Across the Atlantic, from a pay phone in another airport, Ray frantically called the pastor, praying as he dialed. *Lord, please get Janis Smits on a plane.*

"Would it be possible," he had politely asked, "for you to help me with some airfare expenses? It's a bit of an emergency ... If you could call the airline ... Frankfurt to Washington, D.C. The name is Janis Smits ... thank you. I'll be in touch very soon. Thank you so very much."

Hours later, Janis Smits arrived safely in Washington, as did all the others who were scheduled to testify. By the time the hearings actually began, Ray was beginning to feel better. Along with increased physical strength, a sense of anticipation returned. Now, sitting in the large conference room, he was able to observe the awesome political machinery.

House Resolution 726

The hearings couldn't have been more effective. On September 2, 1976, the committee's report was formerly printed:

> *The Committee on International Relations, to whom was referred the Concurrent Resolution (H. Con. Res. 726) to urge the Soviet Union to release Georgi Vins and permit religious believers within its borders to worship God according to their own conscience, having con-*

sidered the same, report favourably thereon without amendment and recommend that the resolution do pass.

The resolution was passed by the House of Representatives on September 20, 1976, by a vote of 381 to 2. And, as part of the last order of business of the Gerald Ford administration, the United States Senate passed the resolution by a unanimous voice vote on October 1, 1976.

The beloved Senator who spearheaded this last-minute effort in the Senate was well-known to all who watched him rushing about, assuring every possible vote. His name was Hubert H. Humphrey.

It was an astounding feat. But it wasn't enough for Ray Barnett. Within weeks he sent Guy Wiggins to London. After another burst of political activity, Motion No. 68, on behalf of Georgi Vins, was passed by British Parliament that same year.

And so it was that two of the most powerful free-world nations joined together in formal protest. As one, they decried the Soviet Union's inhumanity to Christians. In spiritual agreement, they rebuked the U. S. S. R.'s oppression of imprisoned Baptist pastor Georgi Vins.

And behind it all stood an unassuming, somewhat shy man of forty years. He was neither an American nor an Englishman. To that very day, he could not produce a legible written report. Financial matters frustrated him. He sometimes failed to return phone calls. He often left loose ends behind as he rushed toward the goals he set for himself. But the fact remained—because of Ray Barnett, the impossible had been done. And in years to come, State Department veteran Guy Wiggins would say,

"I would have never attempted such a thing on my own. Ray may not have had a great deal of political experience, but despite the odds, he and his little organization were doing everything they possibly could to combat the overwhelming tyranny that reigns within the Soviet Union.

"As for me, it gave me great confidence to know that wherever I went and to whomever I spoke, Ray Barnett was standing behind me. He is a man of unusual personal courage. He always seems to feel that the arms of God are beneath him."

Big Home for a Big Family

In the meantime, during the course of the hearings, Ray Barnett and Janis Smits had become fast friends. The exiled Latvian Baptist minister was living in Germany with his wife, his mother and his twelve children. They had been out of the Soviet Union for less than a month. And since the West German government had only provided them with a one-year visa, a new place of residence would have to be found without delay.

He explained the problem to Ray over coffee one morning: "I don't know where we're going to go," Janis shook his head sadly. "God will have to show us. There are so many in the family. It makes getting permanent visas very difficult."

"Look Janis," Ray smiled. "Why don't you come to Vancouver before you go back to Germany? I'll show you around. Who knows? Maybe I can help you and your family get visas into Canada."

"I have some speaking engagements for the next ten days or so, but maybe after that." Suddenly Janis's eyes brightened, "But that makes me think of something I need to ask you. Do you know of a place in the Northwest part of America called Douglas?"

"Douglas ... " Ray thought for a moment. "No, I don't think so. Why?"

"Oh, well," Janis looked a little sheepish. "I'm not a dreamer of dreams. But over a year ago, while I was still in the Soviet Union, I dreamed of the map of North America. And on the far left side, in the northwest, was the word 'Douglas' circled in red. The dream stayed in my memory. I looked on many maps in days to come, but could find no such place."

Ray smiled at Janis. "Well, you meet me in Seattle in a couple of weeks. After we drive to my home in Vancouver, we'll look on a local map. Maybe we can find Douglas."

"Yes, I'd like to look for it. Somehow it seems important to me."

Ray smiled, took off his glasses and rubbed his eyes. "Just remind me when you get there, Janis. I may not remember otherwise."

Interstate 5 to Canada

After his speaking tour to address Latvian Christians, Janis Smits flew to Seattle to meet Ray. Because Janis had only been in the U.S. for a few weeks, his mind was still spinning with cultural differences. He was physically exhausted and looking forward to a few days of sightseeing in the Northwest.

He and Ray began their drive northward to the Canadian border. The pine-studded scenery was refreshing, and Janis began to relax as they talked. Ray told him a little more about Friends in the West. "Did I explain our Prisoners for Christ bracelets to you?" He held up his wrist, displaying his own Georgi Vins bracelet.

As Janis examined it, Ray quietly said, "Sometimes I can't sleep nights thinking about the man. We've had bracelets made. We've prayed. We've even succeeded in getting resolutions through Congress and Parliament and yet he's just as much a prisoner as ever."

There was silence. The car sped toward Vancouver, but Ray's mind was temporarily focused on a Siberian prison camp and an ailing man thousands of miles away. When their pleasant conversation finally resumed, it centered around the work that was being carried on behind the Iron Curtain and the possibility of Janis's involvement. Ray told of the dreams and goals that were forever turning around in his mind.

At last they arrived at the border. Because he still carried a Soviet passport, it was necessary for Janis to go into an immigration office for a brief interview. Ray waited outside. The officer on duty asked a few polite questions. At last he said, "And how long will you be staying in Canada, sir?"

"Just a few days. I am visiting a friend."

With that, he stamped the passport firmly and returned it to Janis Smits. Janis looked at the fresh ink and caught his breath.

"DOUGLAS" was the name that had been stamped on the page. "Is this Douglas, British Columbia, then?" he asked, electrified at the sight of the long sought name.

"It's not really a city or town. It's just the name of the border crossing. That's all."

When Janis returned to the car, he silently handed Ray the passport, pointing to the stamped name. They looked at each other for a moment, speechless and deeply moved. "So you've found Douglas." Ray finally spoke, marveling at the miracle.

"This is God's way of clearly showing me where He wants me. Now I cannot doubt that it is His choice, and not mine, for me to come to Vancouver."

"There's no doubt in my mind either, Janis. We'd better get started trying to arrange for your visas. It could take quite a while."

"From what I've heard, it's impossible to get Canadian visas for us, Ray. The people I've talked to say it can't be done."

At that moment Ray was hastily making a U-turn. All his attention had been riveted on the astonishing passport incident and he had unintentionally arrived at a dead-end street. Heading back toward the main highway, he laughed abruptly: "Nothing is impossible Janis. Absolutely nothing."

Visas, Airfare and Housing

No one ever really knew how Ray went about getting visas for the entire Smits family. Some attributed it to knowing the right people in the right places. Others simply said "it's another miracle." Whatever the explanation, it was done. And it wasn't long before the time came for the Smits entourage to board a jet and make their way to Vancouver.

This created yet another obstacle. Airfare for fifteen people amounted to around $5,000. There was no such nest egg in the Friends in the West bank account. As usual, the organization was operating on a thin edge. Ray decided to fly to Los Angeles, where fund raising for such a project might prove to be the most successful.

He made appointments with virtually every contact he could possibly remember. He was obsessed with the Smits' dilemma. Someone simply had to help. It was clearly God's plan for the family to come. But where was the money?

Every door seemed to be closed. Ray's feeling of frustration grew as time ran out. He hated to go back to Vancouver without the money for the tickets. A house had been located. Volunteers were already preparing it for the family to move in. And most important of all, the Smits' West German visas would expire within days.

Nonetheless, his final appointment proved fruitless. He dejectedly gathered his luggage and made his way to the airport. He felt exhausted and slightly desperate. God must have some other way of getting them over here. He's not going to let them down this easily. He comforted himself with that thought, checked himself onto his flight and waited to board.

The announcement was soon made that boarding had begun. He sat a moment longer until the rush diminished. Finally he stood up and began to walk toward the gate. "Your attention please ... " The ceaseless paging of passengers was so familiar that at first he didn't listen.

"Your attention please. Ray Barnett. ..Ray Barnett, please go to a white courtesy telephone. Ray Barnett, please."

He grabbed the phone just as the last call for his flight was made. "Hello, Ray? Dean Jones. I heard about your Russian family. The airfare is $5,000, right? Look, I'll take care of it. I'd like to do that for them. God bless you, brother."

Ray hung up, raced up the ramp and barely got onto the plane before the door swung closed. He dropped heavily into his seat, sweating, breathing rapidly and smiling in wonder. *Another minute and I would have gone home empty-handed. Thanks, Lord.*

Even Vandals Can Do God's Will

When Ray arrived in Vancouver, the house that was being prepared for the Smits family was almost completed. "It's better than my house!" he laughingly told a friend who joined him for a last-minute tour.

"How'd you ever find this place, Ray?"

"Well, it belongs to a local church here. It just seemed right for the family, because of its size. It's such a big old house, unusually big for a church property. And you know they have twelve kids and a grandmother coming."

"That's what I heard. So the church said you could rent it?"

"Well, not exactly. They said we couldn't rent it at first. It was vacant, but for some reason they didn't want us to have it."

"So you prayed, right?"

Ray's mouth twisted into a crooked smile. "We really felt it was the right house, so we more or less told the Lord we needed to have it. A few days later some vandals attacked it and made quite a mess." He restrained a chuckle. "After that the church decided it would be better if someone were living there, so they called and said we could rent it."

Even as they talked, men were hammering. Women were hanging curtains. The work was nearing completion, and along with the smell of new paint, a spirit of joyful enthusiasm seasoned the efforts. Most of the participants were from Bible Fellowship, a local church that had wholeheartedly contributed time and money to creating a home for the new family.

At last the day came for the Smits' long-awaited appearance. They were greeted at the airport with flowers, lollipops and the invitation to come to their new home—a home they were the very last ones to see.

The cars that transported them drove slowly up to the big, wood-frame house. It was meticulously painted. Its windows shone clean and bright. The garden was raked and pruned. Breathlessly, almost on tiptoe, they made their way inside.

The kitchen cupboards were overflowing with food. The refrigerator was stocked with milk and meat and vegetables. Every room was fully furnished, spotless and brightened with flowers. Each of the twelve children found a bed of his own, made up with fresh sheets and blankets. There was nothing left undone—only the laughter of a happy, thankful family had been missing. And now, with that, the project was complete.

Janis and Ruth could do little but weep. It was better than a dream come true. It was ordinary people who had done the work, but it was the extraordinary Spirit of God that had inspired them. "Never could there have been a clearer picture of Christian love, of a Christian family that is truly one in Spirit throughout the whole world."

Nearly ten years later Janis Smits' voice broke as he remembered that beautiful welcome. "It was like a dream. It is impossible to talk about that day with dry eyes. And as for Ray Barnett? For one entire year the man devoted himself to us. He was God's instrument in our lives. We will always love him."

During that year of 1977, Ray Barnett was rewarded by the experience of seeing the Smits family settled and at peace. Yet throughout this time, tragedies were emerging within Africa, tragedies too vile to be ignored. Hideous reports about Idi Amin's atrocities seeped out of Uganda. Everyone, everywhere observed the ceaseless East African nightmare. The world watched helplessly. But Ray Barnett was one of those who could not just sit still.

Ray Barnett decided to see if there was anything he could do to help the persecuted people of Uganda.

SEVEN

MIRACLES IN AFRICA AND BERLIN

Late afternoon stretched foreboding shadows across the city. The streets of Kampala were beginning to empty of people, and the uncomfortable mood seemed to deepen with the darkness. Everyone knew the story. Curfew began at sunset, and with every curfew came more killings.

At that time in 1978 Uganda was struggling and bleeding under the violent assaults of Idi Amin's horrifying reign. Like one single, mistreated captive, the whole nation was locked up in a terrifying imprisonment. Every citizen remained uncertain from one day to the next as to his life or his death. And among the most frequently abused groups was the valiant Ugandan Christian church.

Ray Barnett was tensely riding in a dusty taxicab, watching the shadows deepen in the city. For a white man to be out after curfew was simply suicidal. He knew it well. But the hotel he'd checked into hours before had been teeming with Amin's henchmen. There was reason to believe that they knew of Ray's human rights efforts. He would be quickly disposed of should he be discovered.

So, after a brief look around the hotel, Ray had hailed a cab. "There's a Christian boarding-house in Kampala," he'd explained to the driver. "That's where I want to go."

They eventually arrived at a destination. But it wasn't the right one. An overcrowded Muslim guesthouse, familiar to the driver, promised no haven for the weary Canadian passenger. "No, it's a Christian boarding house."

Coarse-leaved banana trees rustled in the humid breeze as Ray's driver eyed him sceptically and screeched back into the street. He obviously had no idea where he was going. Ray sighed and contemplated his next step. He had come to Uganda against the advice of virtually everyone. He'd been repeatedly reminded that people disappeared there with great regularity, never to be heard from again.

Nevertheless, he'd embarked on the journey out of concern for the persecuted church. He'd made the decision to go without knowing one person in the country. Had it been foolhardy arriving in such a spot without a contact? Now he found himself in a very precarious position. *Lord, I hope I'm where You want me to be. Because if I'm not, I'm in big trouble here. I've got to find some Christians. And I've got to get off the streets in the next few minutes.* He prayed silently, his eyes fixed on the surrounding roadways.

Answered Prayer

Every stranger was potentially dangerous. And every person he saw was a stranger. All at once he noticed a young woman walking along the sidewalk, moving toward the cab. Her face was pretty and was softened by a slight smile.

"Stop!" Ray instructed the driver. "I want to ask this girl for directions."

"Hello," Ray spoke to her almost shyly. "I'm afraid I'm lost." He felt a flutter of encouragement at the sight of such a friendly face. "I'm looking for a Christian guesthouse. Would you know of such a place by any chance?"

Amazement flickered in her dark eyes. She looked at Ray carefully as if in immediate recognition. Her smile broadened. "Why, yes! It's run by some friends of mine. I'll come with you to show you the way." With that she got into the cab, and they rushed off in a new direction.

Ray took a deep breath, beginning to relax.

The young woman spoke, "My name is Faith."

And I'm Pilgrim, Ray thought. *I feel like Pilgrim.* Ray's mouth curved in private amusement, but he kept the thought to himself as they drove toward the place Faith had identified as Namirembe Hill. At the top of a gentle slope, Faith told the driver to stop. The newly acquainted passengers got out of the cab and paid the fare. They began to walk together.

"I didn't want him to know exactly where we were going," she explained. "These days you can't be too careful." Although danger was increasing with their every step, there was a quiet confidence in Faith that touched Ray's heart.

Once inside the spotless, whitewashed guesthouse, he was warmly greeted by other Christians. He couldn't quite understand their enthusiastic welcome. Nevertheless, he explained that he had come there to find out what exactly was happening to the Ugandan church. Soon Naomi and Stephen, the young couple who operated the house, sat down across from him. Stephen told Ray Barnett something that simply took his breath away.

"Only yesterday we prayed specifically that the Lord would allow someone to come from America to visit us today. We asked Him to do this so we'd know He hadn't forgotten His Ugandan church. Surely the Lord has sent you!"

Ray's eyes returned Stephen's gaze. He was speechless. *That's an impossible request,* he told himself. *And it's even more impossible to think that I'm the answer.* He was soon to learn that the guesthouse had welcomed no visitors from North America in several years.

Word of Ray's miraculous arrival spread among the Ugandan believers. One by one, distinguished Christian leaders appeared at the guesthouse, greeting him with a sense of reverence and wonder. They eloquently reported incident after incident of Christian bloodshed, of faith triumphant in the face of misery and murder, and of glorious martyrdom.

Finally, all the Ugandans agreed that Ray should attend an underground church meeting the following morning. They insisted that he go, despite his protestations that his presence would endanger them unnecessarily. That worship experience was to change his life forever.

Victory in the Midst of Heartache

A heart-stopping, clandestine ride across the sweltering city delivered him to a furniture factory. The back door of this clever "front" operation led into a banana grove. Behind the banana grove was a house. And inside the house was a Sunday morning church service.

But before he ever laid eyes on the house, before he even left the furniture factory, Ray Barnett heard singing. Joyful singing. He recognized the song, although the voices were drifting across a great distance.

> *How lovely on the mountains are the feet of him Who brings good news ... Proclaiming peace, announcing news of happiness ... Our God reigns! Our God reigns!*

Tears stung his eyes. How could the church be underground when its praises filled the sultry Sunday morning air with their beauty? How dare these brave believers sing with all their hearts? Why were they so happy when injury or death lurked around every bend in the road?

When he entered the service, Ray found an attitude of joy and victory unlike that of any church he'd ever attended. These were rejoicing people. Victorious people. They might die for their faith. But the Spirit that filled them would live on forever.

In the course of the meeting Ray was introduced. Thunderous applause rocked the building. To these faithful ones, he represented the unchanging love of God. His were "the feet of him who brings good news." Ray Barnett was a messenger from their reigning God.

How humbled he felt! Less than forty-eight hours before he hadn't known a single person in this broken, blood stained land. Now he was embraced with warmth and deep affection.

All along he'd believed that it was God who had instructed him to go to Uganda. Now he knew he'd been right. Like so many other unsung heroes in the troubled world, these people were ready to die for their faith.

I have got to do something for these Ugandans. They put the rest of us to shame with their spirit of praise. I don't know exactly what I'm going to do. But there's got to be a way to help turn things around in this country. It was clear that his involvement with the Ugandan church had only begun.

It was also obvious that there was little more he could accomplish during that visit.

A day later, when Ray was in a Christian leaders' prayer meeting in Kampala, he knew all at once that it was time to do something about an altogether different situation. One particular Baptist dissident was ill and in bondage behind the Iron Curtain. For some time, Ray had known what had to be done for Georgi Vins. Now, with a clear sense of spiritual guidance, he knew that the time had come to do it.

Regretfully, Ray Barnett said good-bye to his new East African friends.

"I'll be in touch with you," he promised before he made his way back to Entebbe Airport. He was amazed to learn, upon arrival in Nairobi, that those courageous Christians had managed to phone Kenya. They'd wanted to make sure he'd gotten out of the country alive!

God be with them; they've changed my life. Now maybe I can do something to change theirs. And as Ray's silent prayer rose from his heart, his Europe-bound jet screamed through the Kenyan skies.

Next stop, Berlin. Georgi Vins had been in his Soviet labor camp long enough. And a group of Pentecostals, later to be known as the Siberian Seven, had already been self-imprisoned in the American Embassy in Moscow for sixty days.

The Lawyer from Berlin

As Ray's plane began its final descent toward the wall-scarred city of Berlin, he restlessly thumbed through the airline magazine he'd pulled from the seat pocket in front of him. He seemed to be looking at the colorful pages, but his mind was racing. He pushed his glasses to the top of his head and rubbed his eyes wearily.

What is his name? Why can't I remember his name? He sighed heavily and stared out the window at the scene below. Three years before Ray had been in another plane seat on his way to somewhere long since forgotten. As was his habit, he had spent his waking moments in flight reading everything he could find. On that particular journey, he'd come across a *Reader's Digest* article about an East Berlin attorney.

The story had recounted the capture of U-2 pilot Gary Francis Powers and the diplomatic exchange which had led to his release from the Soviet Union. A skilful East German attorney had made the complex arrangements. After absorbing the information, Ray had been left with the distinct impression that the day was coming when he would need to see the same lawyer himself on behalf of persecuted Christians.

Three days ago Ray had been in the steamy Ugandan capital of Kampala. There, in the unexpected setting of an east African prayer meeting, he had heard a clear, inner direction to fly to Berlin and contact the attorney on behalf of Georgi Vins and the Siberian Seven.

The flight attendant whisked by, checking seat belts. Another announced that the plane would soon be landing. "Please extinguish all smoking materials ... "

Ray was exhausted. This eight-hour trip from Nairobi had come too close on the heels of his transcontinental flight to Africa just a few days before. His body ached. A cold stirred in his chest. *I haven't much doubt but that God has sent me here*, he thought to himself. *But I sure hope I'm right. And how on earth am I going to find out the man's name?*

Finally the plane landed. Ray pulled his hastily packed clothes bag out of the overhead compartment, grabbed his bulging briefcase and impatiently waited for the doors to open. When at last the crowded aisle began to move, he made his way quickly out the door.

An extensive security check came and went with barely a notice from the man. His mind was elsewhere. Anyone who knew him would have recognized the fact that he was studying a problem. And as always, he would eventually resolve it. But to a casual observer, he would have appeared detached, almost strangely lost in thought.

At last he formulated a plan. He phoned the pastor of a West Berlin Christian Fellowship. *I'll begin there*, he proposed to himself. *At least he* can help me get to a hotel. And then I'll try calling a few friends.

Satisfied with the immediate solution, he relaxed a little. When his friend arrived the two men greeted each other warmly. Within hours Ray was in the company of colleagues who shared his vision for assisting the world's suffering Christian community. And by the end of the second day, the attorney's name had come to one of them.

"Wolfgang Vogel! That's it!" Ray beamed with pleasure at the very sound of the words. Within the hour, he contacted the lawyer by phone.

"Yes. Come over. Be here by five tomorrow," he was advised after a somewhat awkward conversation. The office address was recorded. The mission was on its way.

A Trip Under the Wall

Daybreak found Ray rummaging through his cluttered briefcase, searching for a file that he had carried nearly ten thousand miles. It contained a copy of the United States *Congressional Record*. This would document the resolution that Ray had initiated and had seen through the Congress on Vins's behalf. The file also contained a *TIME* magazine article describing the prisoner's plight in his Siberian exile. Ray would present these matters to Wolfgang Vogel. And perhaps something could be arranged.

Ray and another friend, a skilful interpreter, caught the U-Bahn next day as the sun began to fade into an overcast autumn horizon. The orange underground train roared through its mysterious maze beneath the ugly wall and into the eastern sector of the divided city.

Unsmiling border authorities sold the necessary visas, collected the prescribed number of West German marks and handed the men's passports back along with the little blue slip that gave them permission to stay in East Berlin for a day. When they were finished, more time had passed than either of the men had expected.

Out of breath, they emerged from the Friedrichstrasse U-Bahn station and began to look frantically for a taxi. What if they were too late? At last they reached the address Ray had clutched in his hand for half an hour. He checked his watch. Five to five.

A studious-looking woman greeted them. In a business-like fashion she instructed them to take a seat. A couple of other people waited silently with them. Books lined the walls. A few fine antique pieces decorated the room.

By now Ray Barnett was experiencing the familiar peace that often followed him into crises. He had gotten this far. The rest was up to God. "Dr. Vogel will see you now." The words interrupted his thoughts.

Once in the office of the world famous legal figure, Ray found himself face to face with a large, dignified gentleman of middle age. He was a man of few words, but his face reflected a great deal of character. Ray instinctively liked him.

No Other Christians

Through his interpreter, Ray Barnett began to explain his purpose in being there. "I've come on behalf of this man," he laid the *TIME* magazine article about Vins and the *Congressional Record* on the desk.

At first Vogel seemed to misunderstand. "I've had so many Jewish groups come to me before. Too many cooks spoil the broth, you know."

"No, no. You see we're not Jewish. Of course we're sympathetic to the Jews, and with all they've done we can learn a lot from them. But I've come to speak to you on behalf of Christians in the Soviet Union. We are Christians, doing what we can for those who are suffering for their Christian faith."

Ray went on to explain to the attorney about the *Reader's Digest* article and his belief that Vogel could help them. He mentioned the direction from God he'd felt in the Kampala prayer meeting just days before, and his hope that Vins could be rescued through diplomatic means.

Vogel seemed strangely moved. "What you are asking me to do is very, very difficult," he said slowly. "But I will do what I can. So you're Christians. That's very interesting. No one has ever come to me about Christians before."

The words struck Ray like a blow. Why? He asked himself the question a dozen different ways as he and his companion made their way back to West Berlin. Shadowy eastern streets soon exploded into the dazzling lights of the never-sleeping Ku-Damm. Ray saw nothing. His mind was focused on a new puzzle.

Why has no one ever approached him on behalf of Christians before? That seems nearly impossible to believe. It always amazes me the way the Lord leads. In my own thinking, I would have never thought that I'd be the one to speak to him first about these matters. But the Lord always knows what He's doing. He never fails.

EIGHT

AMAZING ANSWERS TO PRAYER

Later that same year Ray sat one day in his Seattle office making last-minute phone calls before he began the two-hour drive back to his Vancouver home. Suddenly a pastor friend charged into the office, completely out of breath. His eyes were shining. "Ray, I think Salu Daka is out of prison!"

Ray looked at his friend blankly. "What makes you think so?" The pastor would have had no personal contact with the case of the young Rhodesian.

"Look at this." He held out his wrist for Ray's inspection. The prayer bracelet he wore with Salu Daka Ndebele's name on it was broken in half.

"How did you break it?" Ray was still puzzled.

"I didn't break it. It split in half just a few minutes ago. I think the Lord is telling me that my prayers are answered. I think he's out of prison, Ray."

"Well, I hope you're right. I really hope you're right!"

When the pastor left, Ray gathered his belongings and headed his car toward British Columbia. As he drove, he began to review the case of the man in the Mozambique prison.

After his risky visit to Maputo, Ray had succeeded in publishing Salu's picture in the world press. He had also produced hundreds of prayer bracelets. But he hadn't stopped there.

In the course of dealing with Guy Wiggins regarding the Congressional Resolution, Ray had made the case of the jailed American missionaries known to the U.S. Government. Hubert Humphrey had responded personally to the situation by using his influence to bring it to the attention of those diplomats who could do something about it.

Through the intercession of such concerned diplomats at the highest level of U.S. government, the American Christian missionaries were released on April 28, 1978.

One of them, Don Milam, subsequently wrote to Guy Wiggins, "Salu is still there. There have been insinuations that the only way for him to be released is to join the ANC and train for military activity against the regime of Ian Smith. Of course Salu is not interested."

Brainstorm in the Night

During this period of time, Ray Barnett's burden for Salu Daka had grown very heavy indeed. Just as Salu had feared, the whites had gotten out of prison and he was still there. Had he given up hope? Did he realize that Ray had not forgotten him?

One night Ray awoke from a restless sleep. Rumpled and weary, he got out of bed with but one thought on his mind. Walking the floor, he considered this new thought: Salu Daka Ndebele had nothing but a Rhodesian passport. And because of strained relations with Mozambique, that was more of a problem than a blessing. But because Rhodesia was a British colony, Salu was eligible for a British passport. And a British passport could be his ticket out of Maputo!

Next morning Ray was on the phone. He was in touch with people in the United Kingdom who could get the job done. A newspaper report was filed on Fleet Street. Soon a British passport was issued. The wheels began to turn.

Diplomat Guy Wiggins was dispatched to London. He went to Parliament. He explained the problems to influential men—men of world importance who could take action. A British citizen was incarcerated in Mozambique! What was this government going to do about it? Once again, the world's political machinery was in motion.

In light of all that, did a broken prayer bracelet really mean anything? Hope flickered in Ray's spirit when he thought about the possibilities. He knew very well that prayer was more powerful than all the world's governments combined.

But two days later the call came through. The Seattle pastor had been right. Salu Daka Ndebele was a free man!

Walking the friendly residential avenues around his Vancouver home,

Ray thought through the implications of Salu's release. The man had been left in prison with nothing but a promise from a stranger. After that, he'd heard virtually nothing. And yet not a day had passed when efforts were not being made for his freedom.

We're all in the same boat. Ray kicked some leaves aside as he made his way along the sidewalk. God gives us promises and starts working in our lives. It may seem for weeks and months and years as though nothing has happened. But finally the breakthrough comes.

It's just a matter of faith. And patience. And believing Him. Just like I told Salu, "I'll never forget you" and I didn't. It doesn't matter how hopeless things may seem while we're waiting. God does what He says He'll do. And He never forgets us.

Looking Back

A few months later Ray was driving toward Seattle one day and thinking back over three years of endeavor. Friends in the West had been a busy place since the Smits family had been comfortably settled. Now Salu Daka had been released from Mozambique, and the time Ray had spent in that part of the world had once and for all focused his attention on the chilling human-rights violations taking place northward in Uganda.

That had led to his initial visit to Kampala, where he had been so joyfully welcomed by the valiant Christians there. How well he recalled the sound of their praises echoing across the Sunday morning silence! By now Amin was on the run, with Tanzanian forces aggressively driving him northward. *Maybe those people will have some peace in their lives now,* Ray thought as he fondly remembered their friendly smiles and warm embraces.

With rain pelting against his car, Ray's thoughts recaptured that past journey. From Uganda, God had abruptly led him to East Berlin. With a wry smile, he recalled his hectic trip behind the Berlin wall to contact attorney Wolfgang Vogel on behalf of Georgi Vins. *It's a wonder we ever found the man, much less made it to the appointment on time.*

That September meeting a year before had led to some correspondence with Vogel. In January, 1979, Ray had written to him, using a friend's name for security purposes.

He had enclosed background material on Georgi Vins, as well as on the Siberian Seven.

A letter in response, appropriately addressed to his friend, had clearly spelled out the dilemma from Vogel's perspective. Translated, it simply read: "Your letter has arrived. When I have an opportunity I will attend to it. This will be very, very difficult. You will be in a position to understand why."

And, from that time on, to Ray's knowledge, nothing had happened. Of course Georgi Vins prayer bracelets had been distributed widely. And Friends in the West had unceasingly reminded their mailing list of faithful intercessors that Vins desperately needed their prayers.

But Ray felt a surge of impatience as he thought about Vins. The man's health was terrible. He could not continue to live if he were not released. Friends in the West had even gone so far as to locate a physician, Dr. William Standish Reed, at Centro Espanol hospital in Tampa, Florida, who would treat Vins at no charge. The doctor had written to Soviet Ambassador Anatoly Dobrynin requesting that Dobrynin intercede to obtain Vins's release so that he could go to the hospital for medical treatment.

But there had been no favourable response. High hopes so often seemed to deteriorate into disappointments. Why?

Ray grew more and more irritated with the course his thoughts were taking. He restlessly peered through the rain-streaked windshield and began to toy with the radio. He tuned into a news broadcast. A couple of incidental stories drifted past his ears, half noticed. Then, all at once his hands gripped the wheel. It was all he could do not to stare transfixed at the radio itself:

Baptist dissident Georgi Vins has just arrived in Washington, D.C. His plane touched down at Dulles Airport moments ago. Forty-eight hours before he had been in a Siberian transport train, on his way to labor camp. This morning he will have breakfast with President Jimmy Carter. Vins's release was arranged by East German attorney Wolfgang Vogel. The well-known prisoner was exchanged to the west for two KGB agents.

Ray was scarcely able to absorb the reality of the radio newscast. *You've done it, Dr. Vogel!* Ray silently congratulated the dignified man on the other side of the world. *And You've done it, Lord. You've answered the prayers of all those people wearing bracelets. Georgi Vins is a free man. I can hardly believe it!*

And how about the man who'd been invisibly responsible for the entire event? How did he feel? Ray was deeply satisfied, humbled and grateful. He was warmed by his own part in the drama, unknown though it was. It was yet another confirmation that the hand of God was clearly upon him.

On to the Next Problem

But as was always his manner, he barely allowed himself to savor the moment. Because of the way his mind worked, because of the way God always led him, he was forever beginning one project before another was completed. And for better or for worse, his job was never done. No matter how glorious and gratifying the accomplishments, his work would never be finished.

And so it was that before he had arrived in Seattle, another question was already stirring in his mind. *What about the second half of the letter I sent to Wolfgang Vogel?* "The second matter is that of seven Pentecostals who entered the U.S. embassy in Moscow at the beginning of June, 1978, requesting exit visas. They are representative, I believe, of about 3,000 Pentecostal families who have requested exit visas. Your guidance in this matter will be respected."

The Siberian Seven. By that time, nearly everyone had become aware of their plight. And now that Georgi Vins was free, Ray could concentrate on them. Perhaps in time, those seven fugitives within Moscow's U.S. embassy would walk upon the soil of the free world, too.

Ideas began to spin in his mind. Before long Ray had arrived at the Seattle office of Friends in the West. By the time he got there, he had mentally moved on from thoughts about Georgi Vins's release to outlining the next step in the Siberian Seven campaign. I've got to get this Siberian Seven campaign rolling, and I've got to do it soon. Those poor families have been in the embassy far too long.

Driving back toward Vancouver, Ray experienced a growing excitement. Maybe he could get some friends to start things moving in the U.K. And as far as North America was concerned, he had lots of ideas: bracelets, petitions, church meetings. His mind quickly listed the best tools of his trade.

I have a feeling I may be going to Moscow one of these days. That wouldn't surprise me a bit. Maybe I should pay those people a visit myself. Who knows what might happen? By day's end a telex had been sent to the Friends in the West mailing list:

URGENT TOP PRIORITY. ..GEORGI VINS ARRIVED IN THE UNITED STATES TODAY. HE WAS EXCHANGED FOR TWO SOVIET SPIES HELD BY THE U.S. GOVERNMENT. THANK ALL FRIENDS IN THE WEST FOR THEIR HELP DATING BACK TO OUR RESOLUTION IN THE U.S. CONGRESS CONDEMNING THE SOVIET GOVERNMENT FOR THEIR TREATMENT OF PASTOR VINS AND URGING HIS RELEASE. THEN LAST SEPTEMBER FOR THEIR HELP IN SECURING THE SERVICES OF A TOP EAST-WEST NEGOTIATOR TO NEGOTIATE HIS RELEASE DIRECTLY WITH THE KREMLIN. HIS FAMILY WILL SOON JOIN HIM HERE IN THE UNITED STATES.

I AM CONFIDENT WE CAN COUNT ON
CONTINUED SUPPORT TO SECURE THE RELEASE OF
THE TWO PENTECOSTAL FAMILIES WHO HAVE BEEN
UNABLE TO LEAVE THE U.S.
EMBASSY IN MOSCOW SINCE JUNE 27, 1978.
RAY BARNETT, PRESIDENT FRIENDS IN THE WEST

That message began aggressive efforts on behalf of the Siberian Seven. Over the many months that followed, Ray continually traveled between Vancouver and London to coordinate efforts to pressure the Soviet government to release the seven. Those travels made Ray acutely aware of the need for a London office.

Home Away from Home

I desperately need a base in London, he sighed a little wistfully one day at the beginning of yet another visit. He tossed his clothes bag on the bed in the cramped hotel room and thought about his needs. As much time as I spend in London, I should have an office with a bed, a phone and maybe a stove so I can make a decent cup of tea. Wearily Ray shoved the clothes bag aside and collapsed on the bed. The phone woke him from a deep sleep minutes later.

"Catherine," he smiled with delight at the sound of her voice.

Years before, after the mysterious meeting with the old fisherman, he had met his sister. He'd learned at that time that for two years she'd been specifically praying to find her lost brother. By now they were close friends.

"I'm here to see what I can do about those Christians in the Moscow U.S. embassy ... Yes, of course we'll have dinner ... No, I won't be here long. But I've always got time for you and Jim."

Their visit was, as always, a pleasant one. And during the course of the evening, Ray told Catherine and Jim about needing a London base for Friends in the West.

"It couldn't be a worse time to think about such a thing," he smiled, mentally ticking off the costs involved in pursuing the release of the Siberian Seven. "But hotel expense is just money down the drain."

Catherine looked at Jim, a hopeful expression fleeting across her face. *The Sutton house!* she thought to herself. *But there's no way Mother would let him use it.* Catherine's adoptive mother owned a large residence in Sutton, Surrey, at London's southern outskirts. Although her mother would probably not be sympathetic to sharing the big house with Catherine's real brother, it was an ideal location.

Better not even mention it. She refolded her napkin, her eyes fixed on the table thoughtfully. She glanced up at the man sitting across from her, remembering their first encounter.

Although he'd sounded more American than Irish, she'd known he was her brother the moment his voice had come through the phone. How her heart had pounded with delight when she realized that he'd sought her out! It was a direct answer to prayer.

His story of the Irish fisherman had filled her with wonder. *He must have been an angel,* she'd told herself, thanking God again and again that the two of them had finally met.

I used to pray that if I ever passed him on the street I'd somehow recognize him. To this day I don't see much family resemblance. But here we are, having dinner together!

The Lord Is Good

Days later, Ray returned to Canada. His efforts on behalf of the Siberian Seven were ceaseless, although financial stress seemed to limit him at every turn.

From time to time, the thought of a London base crossed his mind. But by now such a thing was out of the question. In fact, despite his determination to help the two families in the U.S. embassy, he was once again beginning to question his life's course.

Why is it always so difficult? he asked himself one morning as he drove toward the Friends in the West office. Maybe God isn't blessing us with money because he wants me to do something else. That afternoon he returned home, more discouraged than ever. Nothing seemed to be progressing as far as the Moscow endeavour was concerned. And the bank account was precariously edging toward the red.

He drove up to his family's friendly, two-story house, parked the car in the driveway, and grabbed the mail. Once inside, he sank into the couch and ripped open a small, blue envelope postmarked England. It was addressed in Catherine's familiar handwriting.

"Dear Ray," it began. "I am sorry to tell you that my mother has suddenly died. I am still reeling with the shock of the news." Saddened, he read on.

"But my one clear thought is this. Her residence in Sutton, Surrey, has been left to me. And ever since we spoke eight weeks ago I've somehow known it should be your London Friends in the West base. I never imagined that Mother would pass away so soon. I don't think it's really hit me yet. But Jim and I are in complete agreement about one thing. The Sutton house belongs to you, Ray. You can pick up the keys when you return to London."

Dear God! He sat motionless, transfixed by this latest miracle. *Five minutes ago I was ready to give up. And just when all seemed lost, You touched my life again. How can I thank You?* Later on, Ray called his sister. Catherine's words came across the sea like a message from Heaven.

"First God prepares us," she told him. "Then He brings about His plan. First He prepared me by leading me to pray for you. Then you heard of me and found me. Later He gave me the clear impression that the Sutton house should be yours, impossible though it was. And now, in the midst of my grief, I'm rejoicing because He's fulfilled His plan again. God's timing is an awesome thing, Ray."

"Oh, yes, Catherine. It is a very awesome thing. I want to tell you something, Catherine. Your gift has done far more for me than just providing me with a London base. This has proved to me, beyond the shadow of a doubt, that no matter how difficult things may be, I'm right where I belong. The work I'm doing is God's will for my life. There's just no question about it."

NINE

CLANDESTINE CAMPING TRIP TO MOSCOW

The rented minibus drove slowly along the clean streets. Eager eyes scanned the cityscape, searching for the familiar symbol. All at once the youngest passenger cried out, "There it is! The American flag! That must be the embassy!"

"Good, Rheanne! You've done it!" Ray Barnett smiled happily at his fourteen-year-old daughter. I'm glad she came along, he thought. She'll never forget this trip as long as she lives. By that time he could see the stars and stripes for himself.

As far as the Soviet authorities were concerned, the nine people packed into the bright red van were on a sightseeing trip. But the truth was that they'd arrived in the Soviet capitol with an altogether different purpose in mind. They were there to visit the seven Pentecostal fugitives who were living in the U.S. embassy.

Five thousand Christians from the United Kingdom had signed a banner, writing notes of encouragement and support to the Siberian Seven. Ray and his team were in Moscow to deliver the banner personally.

A History of Oppression

The adventure had begun long before. Friends in the West had been working behind the scenes for years on behalf of the Vashchenko and Chmykhalov families. Ever since Georgi Vins's release, Ray Barnett had focused his attention on the situation in Moscow. The story was well-known by then.

On June 27, 1978, eight members of the two families had travelled to Moscow from their Siberian home in Chernogorsk. They had a written invitation from the U.S. embassy to discuss the religious persecution they had persistently experienced. The one document they lacked, upon arrival at the embassy, was a letter of permission from Soviet authorities allowing them to enter.

When a Soviet guard barred their way into the embassy, they rushed through the door. But sixteen-year-old John Vashchenko did not make it past a strong, violent militiaman. He was thrown to the ground and nearly choked to death. Then he disappeared.

The families huddled in the embassy, refusing to leave until they received word about the missing teenager. Two weeks later the call came from Vera, his older sister. "John was completely black and blue when he returned home. They were merciless in their beating. If they could do that to a sixteen-year-old boy, what will they do to you? Do not leave the American embassy." At that moment the phone was cut off.

And so it was that the seven remaining Siberian believers had stayed in the embassy—prisoners of their own convictions. Years had passed, one by one. Now it was 1981.

A young American, Dr. Kent Hill, was studying in Moscow on a scholarship. Fluent in Russian, he had been invited by concerned embassy personnel to spend time with the lonely refugees. And when he returned to the United States, he had quickly joined forces with Ray Barnett and Friends in the West. Kent's inside information deepened Ray's concern dramatically.

Ray's commitment to do something about the situation in Moscow had led him to create prayer bracelets, develop information and action packets, and put together a slide show that explained the problem to the public.

After his release, Georgi Vins had said about himself and other Russian dissidents, "If everyone had remained silent, we might well have been dead."

This statement intensified Ray's efforts even more. He made contact with Peter Meadows, a magazine editor in England. Along with Danny Smith and journalist Dan Wooding, Peter had organized a "Free the Siberian Seven" committee in England.

It was through this committee that the idea for the banner had been born. That year at a special gathering, 5,000 adults had lovingly signed the

25-foot-long banner. And Ray Barnett had agreed to personally see that the Siberian Seven received it.

Camping Behind the Curtain

It was decided that a group of concerned Christians would make a camping trip behind the Iron Curtain. In early June, after using the Sutton house as a base for the first time, they travelled by boat from Britain to Holland. There they rented a minibus and began the overland drive toward the Soviet Union.

Peaceful, quilt-like European farm fields rolled past the red van's windows. The miles were marked by ancient cathedrals crowning the hills and surrounded by quiet villages. Each member of the little expedition revelled in the wonder of each moment. Theirs was indeed a unique privilege. But an undercurrent of tension began to grip them as they approached their destination.

A whitewashed guesthouse in Czechoslovakia provided their last sleep outside the U.S.S.R. It was there that they followed through with their final plan for smuggling the banner across the Soviet border. First they stretched it out full length and had their picture taken with it, all nine of them together, displaying it proudly.

Then they cut it in half, folded it inside out, and used it to line their grocery boxes. Tins of food, eggs and other supplies rested innocently on top of it. One of the team, Jerry Thurston from Portland, Oregon, drove the van across the Czech countryside late into the night.

Suddenly he saw the blue lights of a police vehicle growing close in his mirror. Everyone stiffened with dread. Had someone revealed their mission to the authorities?

The stern policeman questioned the man as best he could. It became apparent after a few moments that he thought Jerry was driving erratically. Was he drunk? The truth of the matter was, the American had been trying desperately to figure out where he was going. Somehow the team's navigator had directed him onto the wrong road.

At last they arrived at the Soviet border. "You're a day late," a gruff guard informed them, checking the travel schedule they had had to submit. "And now you can't get through until tomorrow. Don't come back till then."

The campers became irritable. After a sleepless night in a sheltered ravine, their van precariously parked at an angle, the nine returned to the border. At that point the search began.

The minibus was virtually taken apart piece by piece. Every article of luggage, every possession, was scrupulously examined. Rheanne's Bible was removed from her purse.

"Oh, you like this book?" The examiner asked the question sarcastically.

"Well, it's a good book to read," the poised girl responded quietly. "It's small and interesting." Rheanne's Bible was coldly handed back to her.

And although every last grocery item was removed from the cardboard boxes, the banner was never discovered! The van and its passengers were allowed to cross the border.

On to Moscow

As the group was escorted to a hotel, they looked at each other uncertainly. Had things been planned properly? There had been so many hitches. Whispered questions began to cause friction. Naturally the Soviet actions came as no surprise to Ray. But the others weren't so sure. And then they faced another obstacle.

No group of that size would be allowed to travel within the Soviet Union without a chaperone. So, at the hotel, a tourist guide was assigned to the van. Pretty, blonde Svetlana joined them, to the further dismay of some of the team members. "We may as well forget the whole thing. How can we get the job done with her along?"

It was true that Svetlana's presence demanded limitations in conversation and action. But to Ray, working within the "system" was nothing new. He simply had to persevere. God would take care of the rest. Of course, convincing the others of that fact was another matter, particularly when private conversations were at a premium.

Meanwhile, Svetlana was obviously disenchanted with such a menial assignment. This odd collection of North American campers was a far cry from some of the luxury tours she had accompanied before.

"Look," Ray said to her one humid, cloudy evening, brushing a hungry mosquito from his arm as he spoke. "We grew up in two different kinds of society. We've been taught to be suspicious of you—to think that you're a KGB informer." Svetlana looked at him squarely and said nothing. He went on.

"And you're suspicious of us. As far as you're concerned, we're all spies. Maybe if we're just open with each other we can be friends. I'll try my best to keep you informed, Svetlana."

The next day they arrived in Moscow. "I wish I could see my boyfriend." Svetlana sadly shook her head. "I haven't seen him in a while."

"Why don't you go ahead," Ray kindly suggested. "I'll cover for you if anyone asks."

And so it was that the team was without their tourist guide on Saturday morning. They hurriedly left the Olympic campsite where they'd spent the night and began to search for the embassy. After Rheanne's discovery of the American flag, they parked the van and went into the embassy's reception area.

Within half an hour they were with the Siberian Seven, presenting them with the banner! As one of the team wrote in her journal:

> To say the least, the Russians were surprised when nine of us walked into their small quarters. After a brief explanation of why we had come, we presented them with a 25-foot-long banner with the names and encouraging messages of thousands of British Christians and the big headline which read,

SIBERIAN SEVEN, WE CARE!

Of course, as we unrolled it, it was apparent the small room was not large enough. The unrolling process continued into the corridor outside. Tears of gratitude flowed as they realized there were thousands of Christians all over the world who had truly not forgotten them.

The small room shared by the Vashchenkos and the Chmykhalovs was about half the size of an American living room. Besides accommodating seven people, it contained two beds, a small stove and refrigerator, a sink, a bath and two chairs.

It was a difficult, unpleasant situation for the seven Christians. But this visit from nine Western friends gave them a new lease on life. Their faces glowed with pleasure at the sight of the banner, and they clung to every word spoken by the deeply moved Friends in the West delegation.

"Can we come back tomorrow? Maybe we could have a little worship service with you," Ray asked Peter Vashchenko hopefully.

After making arrangements with the embassy officials, the Friends in the West delegation was able to return. On Sunday morning, they read together the Scripture for which these people had risked their lives. They prayed in one Spirit to the Lord who had given them strength to bear their persecution. And just before Ray and the others left, they joined hands to sing "Until We Meet Again."

We'll meet again all right, Ray thought soberly to himself as they left the embassy to meet up with Svetlana, who was waiting to show them all the favorite tourist attractions of Red Square. It's one thing to get a banner in. It's quite another to get them out. But with God's help we'll get that done too.

London

Just a few days later, Ray told of the meeting with the Siberian Seven at a huge rally on their behalf in Trafalgar Square in London. Applause continuously interrupted him as he addressed the massive demonstration. The Vashchenkos and Chmykhalovs had been familiar names to him, now they were also his friends. His voice was intense:

> *The families have been trying to emigrate for twenty years. They've suffered more than their share of hardship simply because they refused to compromise their Christian faith. The two families could see no alternative but to leave their homeland in order to live in a place of religious freedom. It is their desire that their children and grandchildren have the opportunity to live in a country where they have the freedom of choice.*

More applause. "Free the Siberian Seven—hostages of conscience!" shouted a number of voices, echoing the message painted on many of the carefully lettered signs. Ray concluded his appeal with a clear call for solidarity.

> *Thousands of free-world Christians must be immediately motivated to take the necessary action to support the Siberian Seven in their efforts to emigrate. We must work. We must pray. We must act—NOW!*

As if an invisible dam had broken, the crowd surged forth, flooding the city streets. With the coming of darkness an all-night prayer vigil began, held directly across the street from the Soviet embassy in London. Each of the seven Christians was represented by a single, handheld portrait. The message was bold and clear.

Watching the scene unfold, Ray felt a certain sense of satisfaction. *This will get the U. K. campaign going again*, he promised himself. *The more press attention we get now, the better chance we have to get things done on* a diplomatic level later on.

But, as is so often the case with such efforts, the excitement soon died down. And the dismal wait continued, unabated by cheers, applause or marching feet. Months passed. Summer turned to fall, and still the families remained huddled in the embassy, looking forward to yet another Christmas in their tiny, drab room.

In December, it was decided that Kent Hill should return to Moscow to visit the seven. Perhaps if he spent part of the Christmas season with them, their sagging spirits would be lifted. Sponsored by Friends in the West, Dr. Hill flew from Seattle to Moscow the day after Christmas. Two days before his arrival, Augustina Vashchenko began her hunger strike. She was joined by her daughter, Lida, a few days later. Although he pleaded with both the embassy officials and the seven, Hill was unable to deter the two women from their fast.

Hope and Hopelessness Together

Ironically, at the same moment the women began their hunger strike, a major breakthrough was made diplomatically on their behalf. Word came from a reliable German source that the Soviet Union was ready to talk.

Helplessly Ray Barnett, Kent Hill and others close to the situation watched Lida and her mother starving themselves. They fervently disagreed with the hunger strike, but understood its impassioned message. If only it wouldn't jeopardize those critical, top-secret negotiations that were taking place! And if only the Siberian Seven could know that hope for their release was beginning to bud!

Before long, Augustina ended her fast. But in February, Ray Barnett and Canadian medical doctor Doug Roberts decided to go to Moscow on Lida's behalf. They hoped to act as negotiators with her as well as with the others.

Friends in the West desperately sought to raise funds for the two airfares. For a time it seemed as if the trip might not be possible. Then at the eleventh hour persistent visa problems were abruptly resolved, and a $5,000 check was express mailed to the Seattle office by Horizon Christian Fellowship in southern California.

Ray and Dr. Roberts arrived in Moscow as Lida's hunger strike reached a perilous stage. It had already been arranged that when she began to endanger her life, she would be taken to a Soviet hospital. All the while, everyone tried to get her to change her mind.

Within days she was moved by limousine to Bodkin Hospital, a well-known diplomatic medical facility. Once she was in the hands of medical experts, Ray took a train from Moscow to Helsinki, Finland. There he contacted the international press. The next morning Lida Vashchenko's picture was on the front page of the *New York Times*.

On the way back to Canada, Ray Barnett and Dr. Roberts appeared on ABC's "Good Morning, America." Their interview with David Hartman reached 50 million homes. Publicity for the Siberian Seven campaign was no longer a problem. Perhaps from now on the free-world negotiators would have the upper hand, Ray thought.

After her release from Bodkin Hospital, Lida was allowed to visit her family in Chernogorsk before returning to the embassy. It was becoming increasingly clear that the Soviet authorities were softening their position with regard to the Siberian Seven.

Ray returned home feeling that very soon the Siberian Seven would be allowed to emigrate to freedom. He felt a quiet confidence that circumstances were moving in the right direction. It wouldn't be long until the publicity might force the families' release.

But all too soon the eyes of the world turned away from Moscow. They focused on another continent, another crisis. Cities whose strange-sounding names fill the pages of the Bible suddenly appeared in the headlines of the world's foremost newspapers.

Determined once and for all to end the terror of the PLO, Israel had invaded Lebanon. The goal was understandable. The courage displayed was admirable. The price paid in human tragedy was beyond comprehension.

TEN

SUFFERING AND RELIEF IN THE MIDDLE EAST

Near Sidon's battered seafront, the exhausted old man picked up a shovelful of debris and painfully moved it toward his left. Sweat streaked his weathered, weary face. Again and again he lifted bits of rubble from one pile to the next, making no evident headway at all. Ray Barnett stood fifty yards away, watching the scene, his eyes stinging with tears.

It's an endless task, clearing those rocks, Ray thought. It's hopeless. Yet he keeps at it. I can't believe the spirit of these Lebanese people. They get bombed out again and again. But they never give up.

By the next morning, Ray had organized a team of volunteers to help the old man. Soon the pile of rubble became a house again. And before they were finished, those same workers had aided thousands of others along that demolished seafront. The fishermen of Sidon were able to live in their homes once again.

Ray's "quick" trip to Lebanon in 1982 had stretched into months. But the endeavour had actually begun in Ray's Vancouver living room. There he had watched Ted Koppel on ABC's "Nightline" reporting on Israel's invasion of Lebanon. Like the rest of the world, he had been troubled by the blockade of relief supplies off the coast of Tyre and Sidon.

Why don't they just take the food and medical cargo in the back way, behind the Israeli forces? He puzzled over the question. Next morning he went to the phone. George Otis, who operated High Adventure Ministries in Lebanon, was on vacation. Ray tracked down his vice president, Fred Johnson.

"You've got to get some relief supplies in there, Fred," Ray challenged him with his concern.

"We don't have any experience in that kind of thing, Ray," Fred had responded. His first reaction to Ray's suggestion was negative. But before long a call was returned by George Otis himself.

"You've managed to ruin my vacation," he told Ray, only half-kidding. "I've had this relief situation on my mind for days. I'll tell you what. We'll give you $5,000 and let you use our van. You'll have to handle the distribution yourself."

From Friend to Relief Organizer

Seventy-two hours later, Ray was on his way to Israel. He arrived in the evening and checked himself into a small frontier hotel. Alone in his room, he listened as war thundered in the distance. Outside, the sounds of tanks and soldiers filled the streets.

Lord, I don't know what I'm going to do here, Ray prayed. *You're going to have to give me some extra wisdom.* He went to the window. Below him was a bustling military scene. Tension tightened within him.

Next morning he was met by a friend from Metulla. After obtaining Israeli army passes to cross the border, the two made their way into Lebanon. What they discovered there could only be described as utter devastation.

Building after building lay in heaps of rubble. Bomb-shattered cement dust clouded the streets. Villages were in absolute disarray. Thousands and thousands of people were desperately reaching out for help. Their problems seemed insurmountable.

Ray felt as if an unbearable weight were pressing against his spirit. What could be done in the face of such need? What could possibly be accomplished with just $5,000?

The next morning he was standing at the hotel counter when a little girl approached him. "Are you an American?" she shyly inquired.

"No, I'm not. I'm a Canadian. How about you?"

"I'm Lebanese," she replied. At that moment a distinguished-looking man joined them. "Her name is Jeanine," he informed Ray, protectively placing his hand on her dark, shining hair.

As Ray talked to the man, he learned that he was one of the first Lebanese refugees who had been allowed to leave their country. He was a professor who, with his family, lived along the main street of Sidon. Like a number of others in the hotel, he was trying to make telephone contact with friends and family abroad.

"I'm here to try to set up some kind of a relief effort," Ray explained. "But at the moment it seems like a pretty insurmountable job."

The professor shook his head sadly in reply. Just then a young man and an attractive woman appeared. "This is my wife, Kathy, and my son, Ronnie," Professor Kherela introduced the rest of his family to Ray. "Listen, I'll tell you what, if you want to help us clear the rubble out of our house, you can certainly use it as a base—if that'll help you."

Thanks, Lord. Ray breathed a sigh of relief. It's a step in the right direction.

The Kherela house had obviously once been quite a lovely home. But now the windows were blasted out. There was debris everywhere. Without fanfare, the new friends began the immense task of cleaning up.

Meanwhile, Ronnie took it upon himself to find a way of turning some of Ray's $5,000 into food. Through his persistence, the van Ray had borrowed was soon loaded with a half-ton each of rice, sugar and flour. And by early morning it was on its way to a mountain orphanage. "Lebanon-Aid" had officially begun.

The $5,000 That Kept Growing

When Ray and Ronnie arrived there, they found that the number of orphans had tripled since the war had begun. And the people had literally been praying for food. Later on, Ray dictated a message to be sent to Friends in the West describing the situation:

> There was the orphanage completely out of food, with 600 hungry mouths to feed. The little children were crying from hunger pains, and the sisters were on their knees desperately crying out to God for provision when our van arrived.

The physical task of unloading the supplies gave Ray a moment for thought. Into his mind flitted the memory of a letter that had recently come to Friends in the West. "Ray, do you know how to move a mountain? You do it a shovelful at a time."

Gradually the orphans were fed. One by one, needs were met. As hours passed, a feeling of deep satisfaction began to strengthen Ray. If I just take care of things as they come, a lot will be accomplished. A little here, a little there. That's how the job gets done.

Ray and Ronnie arrived back at the Sidon house in time for curfew. Just as they were settling in for the evening, a loud knock at the door startled them. A neighbour had risked going out after curfew to tell them of a diabetic orphan girl who desperately needed insulin. Could Ray somehow help?

Next morning he made his way back to Israel and got the child some insulin. Before he realized what had happened, word of his kindness to little Bahasia had spread through the city. As it turned out, the girl belonged to a wealthy Muslim family. Her relatives were well-connected throughout Sidon.

Then came another cry for help—an elderly man needed heart medication. Ray was able to procure it from London. And he was soon to find out that the old gentleman was a former prime minister of Lebanon.

The network of connections was amazing. Because of the Kherelas, Bahasia and the elderly diplomat, the operation grew and flourished. It seemed to have a life of its own. Ray's original $5,000 was never exhausted. Before long sophisticated medical teams were arriving. And, as his special project, Ray erected a tent village for children up in the mountains. War-weary boys and girls went to "camp" for the first time in their lives.

By night, near that mountain retreat, Ray could sometimes be found sitting on a secluded hillside. Slumped in his well-worn Israeli commando jacket, his eyes riveted on the horizon, he'd grimly watch the terrible battles that were shattering Beirut.

Rockets exploded in fiery flashes. Gunfire flared. The sky blazed.

Peet Simonis from South Africa was a journalist friend of Ray's. His poignant words, written after a car bomb explosion, described sights that grew painfully familiar to all the Lebanon-Aid co-labourers:

> *A young boy was standing on the pavement crying bitterly as he and others watched in horror the flames engulfing shops and cars in the heart of the small Lebanese town of Marjayoun. Only the engine and a few pieces of twisted steel remained of one car where it had been flung into a small side street. But in the burning wreckage of a Renault, two people were trapped and already burnt beyond recognition.*
>
> *"Oh, dear Jesus, please help," the director of Voice of Hope radio station in North East Lebanon had prayed aloud as he and I were approaching the scene of blood, tears, hate and fire. Soldiers mingled with the local residents to try to comfort those crying at the scene of sudden destruction.*

Hope Shared

As the battle spread and persisted, so did the relief effort. It moved from Sidon to Tyre and eventually into Beirut itself. Before long, assistance was even taken into Palestinian refugee camps. To many Lebanese, Palestinians were largely to blame for the war itself. But to Ray's view, they were needy people. They were poor. His heart went out to them and with his heart went his help.

One afternoon word reached him that a team from Youth With A Mission (YWAM) had arrived in Lebanon. They were working in a south Lebanese village. When he eventually found the time to meet them, Ray was greeted by an old friend.

With a great surge of excitement, Ray shook hands with the leader of the YWAM operation. He was a small, black man with a fine reputation for hard work and diligence. His name was Salu Daka Ndebele.

Throughout this exhausting period of time, Ray endeared himself to hundreds of grateful Lebanese people. For the rest of their lives, they would remember the countless acts of kindness that he did for them in the midst of the war's devastation. In his Friends in the West letter Ray reported,

> *After the explosion in Tyre that killed so many Israeli soldiers, I was called to the hospital to visit a Lebanese man who was at the site of the explosion and had lost his eyesight. I was there to help him and his family financially, but in addition, I felt prompted by the Holy Spirit to read the Scripture to him about the healing of the blind man and asked him if I could pray the prayer of faith for his eyesight to return. Some time later, he came to me rejoicing. His eyesight was restored, and he was praising God for the miracle. He wanted to be born again!*

Such joyful incidents balanced the ceaseless emotional strain of seemingly endless toil. Toward the end of his tenure there, Ray's heart was touched with a long, awaited delight—his son Rob arrived to join him for a month. To Ray, Rob's presence provided a special kind of companionship. The two of them had always been good friends. As for Rob, the young man had the once in a lifetime opportunity to view that tumultuous part of the world through eyes no tourist would ever possess. He was never to forget people he met. The sights and sounds of war. The world he discovered there.

At last the time came for Ray to move on. He had only been back to Canada three times in the course of a year. Although Rob was with him at last, he missed the rest of his family terribly. He longed to stretch out on his own couch, to eat home-cooked food, to hear about the daily lives of his wife and children. These were small pleasures, but they seemed to grow larger with every day he was deprived of them.

And as months had come and gone, he'd grown aware of another source of inner disturbance. More and more, discomfort gripped him whenever he thought about the Siberian Seven, who still were locked inside the U.S. embassy in Moscow.

I've got to get home, he told himself one afternoon as he stood gazing at the Mediterranean glistening beyond Sidon's war-torn streets. The U. S. campaign to free the Siberian Seven has all but come to an end. And it's not much better in England.

He said goodbye to his good friends the Kherelas, to the volunteers who had tirelessly stood beside him, to the many, many others who tearfully embraced him as they parted. "I'll see you again," he promised them all.

Making his way toward the Israeli border and the jet that would soon carry him homeward, he thought back across the months. We've accomplished a great deal here, thank God. We really have. But it seems to me that others can handle things from here on. I've got to get back to my family. And something's got to be done about those people in Moscow. As far as I'm concerned, they've been in the embassy long enough!

Detour to Vienna

Yet the Mideast efforts would not, in fact, let Ray stay home for any lengthy period of time. Before long, the work required another personal visit, and he soon found himself unlocking the door to the Sutton house which was his U.K. base. He had stopped in London on his way back to the Middle East.

This house is such a blessing, Ray thought as he entered the peaceful front hallway. A restful silence greeted him. Laying down his belongings in an airy upstairs bedroom, he looked out across the back garden, absorbing its tranquil loveliness. Roses were budding. A thousand birds all seemed to be singing with one voice.

Tomorrow he would leave for Tel Aviv. Then, he hoped, he could give his full attention to the continuing dilemma in Moscow. Feeling sleepy, Ray made himself a pot of tea, relaxing in the solitude. All at once the phone rang.

"Ray, I'm glad I tracked you down." It was a friend from Yakima, Washington. Drowsy with jet lag and puzzled by the call, Ray almost missed the man's next statement. "I just heard on the radio that Lida Vashchenko is on a flight from Moscow to Vienna. Is that true?"

"I don't know," Ray replied, suddenly wide awake. "But I'm sure going to find out."

In a flurry of excitement, Ray began to make calls. The report was confirmed. He quickly changed his reservations from Tel Aviv to Vienna. With a feeling of near disbelief, the next day he met the young woman there. It was April, 1982. She had entered the embassy in Moscow nearly four years ago. At last Lida Vashchenko was free!

"I want to go to Israel," she informed him as they talked in Vienna. "I have the choice of going either there or to Germany. But Israel is where I wish to live."

"Do you know what you'll do when you get there?"

"Not exactly. But I know that's where I want to go."

Ray's mind raced. If she'd chosen to go to Israel a year before he couldn't have helped her at all. But now he had more than enough contacts in the Middle East to settle her comfortably. Even more amazing was the fact that he was already on his way there!

As they stepped off the plane in Tel Aviv, they were met by a flash of cameras and a hustling entourage of television reporters. The media was out in force. An impromptu press conference had to be given.

The next morning Lida Vashchenko's picture was on the front page of newspapers all over the world. She was instantly a celebrity, and her story of liberation touched the hearts of millions. It was a time of great ideological triumph, but Ray sensed that on a personal level Lida needed to find a place of peace. Her spirit was crying out for a private haven where she could pray and think.

He knew of a small hotel overlooking the Sea of Galilee and arranged for her to stay there. From her room she was able to look out her window at the very places where Jesus had walked. She could see the beaches where He had preached. She could look across the shining waters where He had sailed with His disciples, filling their empty nets with fish.

No less profound was the miracle of her freedom. Faith told her that the same Jesus who had once performed signs and wonders in this beautiful land of Israel had set her free from captivity, once and for all. Like His first disciples, she had chosen to follow Him. "I will never leave you or forsake you," He had promised. And He had clearly kept His word.

More Travels

Despite Ray's hopes for her privacy, and in spite of the tranquil setting, those were intense days for Lida. Overlooking the brilliant sea, she spent hours on the phone, receiving calls, arranging interviews, and fielding questions from reporters around the globe. Ray took as much of the load upon himself as was humanly possible. But it was an exhausting time.

Then word arrived that the other six Christians in the American embassy were being asked to leave in order to apply for exit visas. They had been told to go home to Chernogorsk and to wait there for their visas to be processed.

"There is no way we will do so until we hear from Lida in Israel," they'd informed the authorities. "Until we receive an invitation to join her there, we will not leave the embassy."

An international phone call became imperative. Connected through Switzerland, hooked up to Moscow across thousands of miles, at last the conversation took place. It was an electrifying moment. From the very land where Jesus had first announced to mankind that He had come "to proclaim liberty to captives," the word was given. Six of His twentieth-century followers were told that the end of their captivity had come at last.

Due to the enthusiasm of the press, public interest in Lida's release did not abate for weeks. The rest of the family joined Lida in June. Ray was able to help introduce them to friends in Nazareth. Touched by the kindness of so many new acquaintances, the families gratefully began a new way of life.

But Lida longed to go to America. She wanted to see the United States and to meet some of the people who had made her release possible. Ray brought her request up to a representative of the U.S. State Department.

"How are you going to keep the trip quiet?" he was asked.

It was clear that the political implications of the Siberian Seven's release required a great deal of care and consideration. The fragile international situation needed to be handled with a delicate touch. Nevertheless, there was another reason for the American government to disallow such a journey.

"I won't tell anyone if you don't," Ray informed the concerned diplomat.

Soon Ray Barnett and Lida Vashchenko were able to make a trip to the United States unannounced. They travelled everywhere and met with hundreds of supporters and friends.

Those who had worn prayer bracelets, those who had written letters, those who had given of themselves financially—all were able to see the young woman with their own eyes. They were first-hand witnesses to answered prayer, and their lives would never be the same.

Within weeks Lida Vashchenko returned to Israel. The world press never knew that the American visit had taken place. And Ray Barnett could return home again—until his next emergency trip.

A few weeks later he was driving to a pastor's conference in Vancouver. He had been invited to speak about the relief work in Lebanon. As he made his way across Vancouver, he reviewed his planned message. The car radio played unnoticed in the background until the words of a news report caught his attention: "In Northern Uganda the German Red Cross estimates that over 100,000 orphaned children are starving to death."

Uganda. Ray's thoughts carried him back to that far-off East African nation. He had loved her warm hearted, joyful people. Uganda's radiant children had touched him so deeply that he'd often wished he could take a choir of them into Russia, to share their exuberance with the suffering

Christians there. Now a portrait of pain filled his thoughts. To no avail he tried to brush it aside.

Could it be true that some of those very children were dying of hunger? A hundred thousand orphans. Lord, I've got to do something. He absently parked his car and rushed into the church hall where the meeting would be held. It can be no coincidence that I heard that report on my way to this pastors' conference. They may think they are going to hear about Lebanon, he told himself as a colleague extended a friendly handshake. But by the time I leave here they are going to know about the situation in Uganda. And with God's help, maybe these pastors and I will find a way to save some children's lives.

ELEVEN

EXTRAORDINARY PRAYERS AND PROMISES

The late afternoon sky was stained scarlet by a sinking sun. Once Makerere's well known little church had been surrounded by Idi Amin's blood-thirsty army, shooting and shouting insults at the Christians inside. But that summer day only childish laughter and singing could be heard outside the simple structure. Along with an odd assortment of friends and relatives, what seemed like hundreds of eager boys and girls had formed a line. Each was awaiting a turn at the "audition."

A sultry wind rattled through the trees. Inside the church building Cindy Kilburn wiped the perspiration from her face and looked with puzzled eyes toward the door. She could've sworn she'd seen this child before … Soon her suspicions were confirmed. Everyone understood that she could only select thirty children for the African Children's Choir. So those who weren't chosen were simply going back to the end of the line, determined to be picked the second or third time around.

Cindy sighed. She was exhausted. More than five hundred children had showed up, having heard about the new choir by word of mouth. How could she possibly say no to so many? They were all beautiful. And nearly every one could sing, and sing well. Ray had been right. It's no wonder he wanted to have a Ugandan choir. She had never heard anything like it! How could there be so many naturally gifted children in one little community?

Cindy was a volunteer, working for a new relief organization specifically created for Uganda's orphans. "Ambassadors of Aid" was based in Vancouver, British Columbia. It had been developed by the group of pastors Ray had addressed months before at a luncheon. They had agreed to stand with him in his vision to help the East African children.

Another New Effort

After the pastors' conference, Ray had flown to Uganda to find out just what needed to be done. At first, he had simply wanted to investigate the problem of starvation. He was taken by armed guards to a refugee camp. And what he found there was heart-breaking.

"It's almost as bad as Belsen and Auschwitz," a grim-faced British companion muttered to himself.

Later on, Ray surveyed a public orphanage. And that was when the decision was made once and for all. The orphans are my first priority, he told himself as he watched them sleeping, curled and cramped into a shell of a building. Some were huddled in tents outside. None of them had more than the clothes on his or her back. It was evident that they were not well fed. And these were the lucky ones.

Several churches agreed with Ray's plan to bring an African Children's Choir to North America. These churches would provide prayer support for the effort. But two men in particular did more than pray. Kirk Duncan and Don Shilton threw themselves wholeheartedly into raising funds. And because of their dedication, a team of volunteers had arrived in Uganda to bring back the choir.

Cindy was accompanied by her mother, Mary Pattison. Dorothy Williams, a former missionary, joined them. Soon Cindy's husband, Al, arrived also willing to lend a hand.

The work was not without its headaches. Besides the vast number of children who showed up, there were the parents who literally begged the team to take their offspring. Many of them widows, the mothers were desperate. It might be the last chance they ever have to eat good food, to wear decent clothing, and to receive an education.

Meanwhile, passports had to be acquired. Visas had to be obtained. Neither would be a trouble-free task. Still, everyone agreed. It would be well worth the effort to gather the children, get them on a jet and present them to the world. The potential of such an endeavour was evident to all.

But the worst obstacle was an unanticipated one.

Two Narrow Escapes

In the midst of an intensive fund-raising campaign in Vancouver, a surprising phone call had reached Ray Barnett. A Russian family whose emigration Friends in the West had been seeking for years urgently needed assistance. It seemed that Ivan Gorelkin, his wife and four children were stranded in Turkey. They had somehow managed to escape from Russia across the Soviet-Turkish border!

Ray rushed to Istanbul. The Gorelkin family greeted him with tears and gratitude. The report they gave of their escape was like a Bible story—an astounding series of spiritual signs and wonders. They accepted Friends in the West's financial gift with great appreciation. Until Ray came, they hadn't had enough money to purchase even a postage stamp.

Then just as he was about to leave Turkey, Ray received another phone call, this one from Uganda. "Ray, Cindy and Al are under house arrest! Their passports have been taken by soldiers. You need to get here as soon as possible."

Uganda was in no way a place to be detained without a passport. The dangers were obvious. "I'm on my way."

After assuring the Gorelkins that he would do all he could for them, Ray rushed up the ramp to board a jet for Frankfurt. From there he flew to Nairobi and caught the next flight to Entebbe.

God help them. Cindy and Al have worked so hard. And now this. Please intercede. We need Your help, Father. Today. Ray's prayer was repeated a dozen different ways throughout the course of his return to Uganda.

At last he arrived in the house where the young couple was staying. In total exhaustion, he collapsed into a chair. "Are you all right? What's happened?"

No sooner had they begun to relate the tale of their unreasonable arrest, than a knock was heard at the door. There stood a sheepish Ugandan official. Almost without a word, he handed Cindy and Al their passports. The crisis had ended. Prayer and a very important woman with influential connections had done the job. A public apology was made the next day.

With that settled, Ray went to check on the children. He soon learned that their passports, which could have taken weeks to process, had been signed off inexplicably in just a matter of hours. A final brief snag occurred when medical exams prevented their receiving Canadian visas. But along with all the other Christians involved, the children had given themselves to a day of prayer. The very next morning, they all passed their rescheduled medical exams without exception, even though malnutrition had largely contributed to their less-than- acceptable health!

Ambassadors to Disneyland

In September, 1984, the choir finally arrived in North America. Before the end of the year they had made countless public appearances. They sang along with *Sesame Street*'s Big Bird accompanied by the Vancouver Symphony. They performed on television, on the radio, at Disneyland and Knott's Berry Farm.

And with the money they raised, Ambassadors of Aid opened the Makerere Children's Home less than a year later. Thirty more children were brought in. The fulfilment of the vision had begun.

That same September, like a reminder of his primary calling, Ray also welcomed the Ivan Gorelkin family to Canada. They had received a Ministerial Permit from the Canadian Minister of Immigration. All medical examinations and visas had been waived.

They came with only the clothes they wore and a matchless testimony of God's unchanging faithfulness. He had promised them deliverance. Loved ones and Friends in the West had prayed. And now, there they were—safe in Canada. Soon they were settled in a house with furniture, clothing and enough money to get started in their new life.

On a December Sunday, Christmas lights shimmered in the wet streets outside a crowded church. Ray stood inconspicuously in the back, listening to the voices of thirty beautiful black children, their faces glowing with happiness and health.

They hardly look like the same kids we brought over here three months ago, Ray thought.

"He's got the whole world in His hands." The familiar words rang through the sanctuary, borne on wings of joy. *How true,* Ray thought, reviewing the extraordinary events of the past months. *He does have the whole world in His hands. These children with their hope for the future. The Gorelkins with their saga of miracles.*

My life, too, with all its unexplainable directions and detours. I never imagined myself guardian over thirty little children. Ray smiled at this peculiar twist in his path. *But what else could I do? And as far as the future is concerned, who knows?*

He certainly does have us all in His hands. And He's not finished with us yet, either. I wonder what will be next on God's agenda for me?

Another New Direction

As usual, Ray didn't have long to wait before God revealed what new road was open to him. Over the next year and a half, Ray continued his efforts in Africa, the Mideast and the Soviet Union. But one day in 1986 a daily news report struck him like a brick.

He and his family were gathered in their living room, talking quietly during the news, when one report caught Ray's attention:

> *Glenn Anderson, brother of Terry Anderson, one of the American hostages being held in Lebanon by the Islamic Jihad, has died. Two days ago he made a desperate appeal to his brother's kidnappers, pleading with them to release his brother so that he could see him before his imminent death. Glenn Anderson's death ends his battle with cancer.*

Terry and Glenn Anderson's father also died recently. He, too, was a victim of cancer, dying during his son's captivity.

Ray left the room abruptly, his eyes welling with tears. He had seen Glenn Anderson's recent deathbed appeal to the Islamic Jihad. Now the man's last hope to see his brother had died with him.

Because of his lengthy involvement in Lebanon, the American hostage problem there had frequently troubled Ray. It had always seemed as if he might be able to do something on their behalf. Now, early in the summer of 1986, this Anderson family tragedy had brought him face-to-face with the fact that he needed to act. But how could he possibly help?

Friends in the West had always been concerned with suffering people. However, the ministry had traditionally reached out to persecuted Christians—people who were being mistreated because of their faith. This hostage crisis was clearly not the same kind of situation. And yet Ray had felt this kind of inner direction so many times before. He knew God was urging him on. He would have to obey.

Ray picked up the phone and called one of the Friends in the West staff members in the United States. "I want you to see what you can find out about these hostages and their families. And once you get the names and dates and the dates of the kidnappings correct, will you order some prayer bracelets?"

New Names for Prayer

The research began. Names were compiled. Calls were made. "We're a Christian human-rights organization. Would you object to a prayer campaign on behalf of the hostages?"

In every case, the families gratefully said, "Yes! Of course we'd welcome a prayer campaign." Eric Jacobsen, David's son, later reported in a Southern California newspaper:

I was at Mass one Sunday, and I was just really depressed, close to the breaking point. I was praying, and I was saying, "Father, I've just had it up to here. It's in Your hands."

The next day, I received a telephone call from a representative of Friends in the West, a Seattle-based Christian human-rights organization. The group offered to organize 24-hour-a-day prayer chains. Prayer bracelets bearing the names of the hostages were distributed.

As Eric spoke to Friends in the West, he explained that his father had become a committed Christian three years before his kidnapping. In one of the two letters David was able to send to his family, he said, "Please love one another. Trust in the Lord ... Coming to the Lord has made it possible for me to survive."

Peggy Say, hostage Terry Anderson's sister, told of her brother's return to his Catholic faith. "We are told that Terry and David Jacobsen are roommates ... They both lost their glasses in the kidnappings. Day after day, Terry held the Bible about three inches from his eyes and read it aloud to David ... Faith in God is our greatest hope."

Major newspapers reported the prayer campaign. Over ten thousand letters were sent out. Millions of people were called to prayer through interviews on international radio and television broadcasts. Thousands of bracelets were distributed. A guest column in *USA TODAY* allowed Friends in the West to remind the nation that prayer provided an answer to their sense of helplessness regarding the hostages. When hundreds of Christians were officially called to prayer on July 4, 1986, no word had been heard of the Lebanon hostages for eight months. Within three and a half weeks, Father Lawrence Martin Jenco, a Catholic priest, was released by the Islamic Jihad. The hostage crisis hardly left the papers from that time on.

The Most Powerful Force

While seeking to mobilize millions of prayer warriors, Ray traveled to the Middle East several times. Between two of those trips, he and Ruth paused to commemorate twenty-five years of marriage. Their three children surprised them with a festive reception. And when Ray returned to the Lebanon crisis, he went with his heart warmed by the love of his family and friends.

"Prayer is more influential than politics," he explained again and again. "Prayer is more forceful than terrorism. Prayer is more powerful than the greatest armies on earth. The prayers of people worldwide will bring our captives back to America."

He met with the Beirut doctors. He met with old acquaintances and new contacts. He met with Patriarch Hakim. Days passed into months.

On October 5, 1986, a group of believers gathered for prayer at Calvary Chapel in Lake Arrowhead, a small mountain community in southern California. Paul and Eric Jacobsen and their wives were there. Ray went to speak on behalf of Friends in the West. An NBC network news crew arrived to videotape the service.

Eric sang the song, "When the Word Comes," which he and his brother had composed. He and Paul showed slides of Lebanon and explained the political circumstances there. They played a videotape of their father which specifically asked pastors to call their churches to prayer, as well as appealing to the U.S. government for action. When the service was about to end, several people prayed. Then the pastor led the worshipers in a simple song from the psalms:

> *Give ear to my words, O LORD,*
> *consider my meditation, Hearken*
> *unto the voice of my cry, my*
> *King, and my God: for unto thee*
> *will I pray.*

*My voice shalt thou hear in the morning,
O LORD; in the morning will I
direct my prayer unto thee, and
will look up. (Ps. 5:1-3, KJV)*

Everyone chose to do just that—to look up in the midst of agonizing circumstances. The family was lovingly brought before the Lord. David Jacobsen was led into the presence of God through the caring prayers of his extended Christian family. A sense of hope warmed the little chapel, fending off the chilly wind that howled around the corners on that autumn night.

"Faith," Paul Jacobsen had explained during the meeting. "I'm beginning to understand faith. Faith means you have what you want while you're still asking for it. Faith means that you can start thanking God for what He's done before you really see it. Faith means that my father is already free."

As it turned out, by the Word of the Lord, David Jacobsen received a message of freedom on that very day. "Dave," the Lord awoke the hostage on October 5, 1986, a clear impression in his mind. "You are going to be free. You'll be released on a morning of the first weekend in November."

Faith was becoming a reality to father and sons alike. And, as He always does, God kept His promise.

TWELVE

WONDROUS THINGS HAPPEN EVERY DAY

For months the words had been carefully written across the Barnett calendar: "Rheanne's wedding." Finally the day had arrived: November 1, 1986.

A portrait of quiet beauty, Ray's twenty-year-old daughter walked down the aisle on the arm of her proud father. With her sister, Rhonda, beside her as an attendant and her brother, Rob, as the host of the reception, it was a day to remember.

On the very same night, the African Children's Choir sang for more than six thousand people at the Shrine Auditorium in Los Angeles. McDonald's Corporation had invited them to perform as the guest choir at their annual Gospelfest. By nine that evening the entire audience was standing, cheering and weeping over the music and message of the little folk from faraway Uganda.

No question—that was an important day for Ray Barnett. And as if those two exciting events weren't news enough, there were persistent reports out of the Middle East that the American hostages might be released within twenty-four hours.

The hostage families responded with a mixture of hope and scepticism. Near midnight Ray went to bed, satisfied that his daughter had enjoyed a glorious wedding day and aware of the choir's rousing success in California.

At 6 A.M. the telephone awakened him. "David Jacobsen is free! He's in Beirut. It's official. He's been released!"

"I'm not surprised," Ray sleepily replied, grateful that the California family would be reunited in time for the holidays.

When the Jacobsens were finally together at Wiesbaden, West Germany, David first heard about the Friends in the West prayer campaign.

On the balcony there he saw his children remove their prayer bracelets and happily throw them to the applauding crowd of reporters below.

He read a bracelet's inscription: DAVID JACOBSEN, May 28, 1985. Along with the name and date he saw the New Testament Scripture reference: "Hebrews 13:3: Remember those in prison as if you were imprisoned with them." And David Jacobsen, better than anyone else, understood its meaning.

"Don't forget the others," David reminded the reporters and well-wishers at Wiesbaden. Later he said, "In many ways I remain imprisoned with Tom Sutherland and Terry Anderson."

Church of the Locked Door

In the days following his release, Jacobsen described an amazing spiritual bond among the men who had shared his captivity.

After being chained to the floor for some months, he eventually was put with four other Americans, the Reverend Benjamin Weir, a Presbyterian minister; Father Jenco, a Catholic priest; Terry Anderson, Beirut Bureau Chief for the Associated Press; and Thomas Sutherland, Dean of Agriculture at the American University of Beirut.

Each of those men had a different perspective on Christianity, with varying backgrounds in the religious community. But very quickly and with great joy, they had organized their own church. They prayed together. Read Scripture together. Took Communion together. Weir and Jenco preached sermons.

Everyone participated in intense discussions. Twice a day they gave full attention to the message of their Bibles—Bibles that had been inexplicably provided by their captors.

Their worship times soon became the high point of their days. They even gave their church a name: "The Church of the Locked Door." And they vowed that once they were all free, they would meet together one last time before the little fellowship was forever disbanded.

In September, 1985, Benjamin Weir was released. Seemingly endless months followed, and the remaining four spent countless hours reading the Bible. Sometimes David would softly sing to himself a worship song he had learned before his kidnapping:

One thing have I desired of the LORD,
that will I seek after;
that I may dwell in the house of the LORD
all the days of my life, to behold the beauty
of the LORD, and to enquire in his temple.
(Ps 27:4, KJV)

Those words came from the text of the 27th Psalm, a Scripture that was to be David Jacobsen's anchor during the turbulent times of his captivity. More and more he could see that only one thing was to be important to him. He was simply to desire to be in the presence of God. What a blessing it was, in such a dreary, cheerless environment, to concentrate on the beauty of the Lord. What a comfort to turn to Him, inquiring of Him for wisdom and encouragement.

But there were more treasures in that same 27th Psalm. The thirteenth and fourteenth verses began to speak clearly to David's heart, particularly after Fr. Jenco's release in July, 1986. The Psalmist rejoiced,

I believe that I shall see the goodness of the
LORD in the land of the living! Wait for the LORD;
be strong, and let your heart take courage; yea,
wait for the LORD!

"Dave," the Lord seemed to be saying. "You are going to be free once again. Just wait and don't be afraid. I've got your life well under control."

The Media Endangers the Man

On September 19, 1986, the kidnappers became extremely angry with Jacobsen due to some speculations made about him by an American network news report. At that point he was isolated from the other prisoners and placed in solitary confinement. He later said, "Everything was removed from me except the plastic bowl I used for my food, my water jug, my underwear and the mat I slept on. At that point I lost all freedoms but for two—the freedom to think and the freedom to pray."

On October 4, his Bible was finally returned to him. He read it hungrily, holding it up to the light that radiated from a hallway bulb. Then, on the morning of October 5, he awoke with an overwhelming awareness that God had given him a promise: "You will be released ... the first weekend in November."

This message from the Lord was so clear that David started a personal countdown to freedom. His Bible was removed again that same day, October 5, and was not returned until the 26th. When it was given to him, Jacobsen eagerly began to read by the weak hallway light. But frustration set in again when the guards abruptly came and "borrowed" his precious light bulb from the hallway. That left him in near darkness once more, making reading an impossibility.

Nevertheless, the Lord calmed him. "Be patient, Dave. They'll bring it back." He obediently quieted himself. And his faith was rewarded. Some hours later, the light bulb was returned. But the next day the light bulb was removed again. And somehow he had less patience that time.

"I want a light bulb!" he complained to the guard. And the guard tried to help him. But the light bulb he came up with was worse than the darkness. It was a fluorescent one, and combined with the unstable electrical current, its flickering beam was absolutely useless.

Once again, Jacobsen couldn't read a word. "Dave," the Lord gently reprimanded him, "I told you to be patient. If you'll just keep faith, they'll bring back the good light. And if you'll trust Me, I'll get you out when I said I would."

It was true. Before long the guard returned. "You need THIS light!" he said, screwing in the original bulb. David Jacobsen was stirred by a deep, swelling hope. If he'd really heard the Lord—and apparently he had—his captivity was nearly over!

At bedtime, November 1, he lay down to sleep at around midnight. Just as he began to doze off, someone came into the room, someone he'd never met. As always, he was blindfolded so he couldn't see the man's face. But the words he spoke were the very words David expected him to say.

"Mr. David," he gently told him. "You are going home in three or four hours."

And so it was that on Sunday, November 2, 1986, David Jacobsen walked through West Beirut, enjoying the sight of the Mediterranean Sea gleaming in the autumn sunlight. Once again David Jacobsen was a free man.

God, Arms and Friends in the West

The days to come were to bring an unprecedented uproar in the world news. "Arms for hostages!" was the outcry. The gaze of the public was moved from hostages to guns to the White House to the Contras in Central America. No one was sure of anything.

David Jacobsen was sure of just one thing: the Lord had promised him that he would be out in the first days of November. And he was. That's all he needed to know just then.

Meanwhile, through the months of his captivity, the prayer campaign had continued in Lebanon as well as in North America. The Lebanese Muslim community had also faithfully pursued its efforts on behalf of the Americans, particularly on behalf of the administrator of the American University Hospital. Ray Barnett had been in almost constant contact with the man from West Beirut. That man had made many a trip to Baalbek, pursuing all possibilities with the Islamic Jihad.

On November 3, 1986, Ray Barnett received a telegraphed message from that young Muslim. "DEAR RAY BARNETT, OUR BEST RE-

GARDS AND OUR WARM REGARDS TO YOU AND TO YOUR FAMILY FRIEND. FOR THE VERY WELL RECOVERY. FOR THE GOOD HEALTH."

Another telex, dated November 5, simply said, "DEAR RAY, TRY TO UNDERSTAND OUR HARD WORK WE DID IT! OUR BEST REGARDS TO YOU AND TO YOUR FAMILY FRIEND."

Was it true? Ray smiled to himself as he considered the tangled circumstances in the Middle East. Who could know? His Middle Eastern friends were obviously convinced that they'd somehow contributed to David Jacobsen's freedom. Ray himself might never be sure.

But one thing was clear. God had unquestionably led him to organize a prayer campaign for the American hostages. Without even realizing it at the outset, he had learned that the hostages were in fact "brothers in bonds," praying, singing, and seeking God's help in their imprisonment. As it had turned out, the Church of the Locked Door was, for all practical purposes, a persecuted church like the others Friends in the West had helped.

At his first press conference, David Jacobsen proudly displayed two Friends in the West prayer bracelets on his wrist. The Associated Press photograph of his upraised arm circled the globe. He placed bracelets on the arms of friends, family members and celebrities. He called an ABC radio talk show and asked the listeners to write for bracelets. He talked about them on national television shows, encouraging everyone to pray.

Finally, he wrote to Ray Barnett:

God bless you for your love, concern, and great efforts. Without you and the Lord I would still be in Lebanon. Although I am now a free man, I will be in chains until Tom, Terry, Joe and the others are released. I plan to work with all my energy to this end. Thank you again for your efforts and the kindness that you have shown my family.

God bless you. I am praying with you as we all continue to "Remember those in prison as if imprisoned with them."

And there'll always be someone. Ray folded the card thoughtfully and looked across the frosty fields that stretched beyond his office windows. As long as there is spiritual conflict in the world, there will be imprisoned Christians. And as long as there are imprisoned Christians, it will be my job to see that they aren't forgotten.

The Tasks Continue

Ray's work did indeed continue. In some ways, his life after Jacobsen's release seemed more hectic than ever. He went to Southern California to record some radio broadcasts.

Another Ugandan choir was touring the Southwest United States, and advance publicity was becoming more and more important.

By then the African Children's Choir was becoming known to many North Americans. Several popular television broadcasts had featured them. Magazine and newspaper articles had been written. Respected leaders had endorsed their ministry.

One choir was in Europe, in the midst of an intensive educational program. They had travelled extensively in the U. K., enthusiastically carrying their message to that part of the world. Soon several of the older children in that choir would return to Uganda.

They would be replaced by a small, lively group of newly selected children about to embark on their own adventure of a lifetime. And so the cycle would continue.

As Ray drove home from the Seattle airport one day early in 1987, he thought about the future. Trees in the Northwest were cloaked in ice. Spring was months away. Another season, another passing year. What lay ahead?

Stopping in Blaine, Washington, Ray removed the mail from his post office box there. Among a number of other letters and cards was a packet of information from a friend.

The Orton Dyslexia Society ... he read the words silently. To him they represented a whole new direction of thinking—a perspective that he'd only gained within the past year or two.

"Did you ever think you might be dyslexic?" a co-worker had asked him one afternoon, trying to understand some of the difficulties he always encountered in writing and mathematics. "Some dyslexics can read well, you know."

Gradually, he began to explore the possibilities. And what he'd learned had changed the course of his life. Virtually every difficulty he'd encountered since his first day of school as a small boy in Coleraine could be traced to a particular set of symptoms broadly identified as "Specific Learning Disabilities."

Testing confirmed without doubt that he was dyslexic and had an attention deficit disorder. These two disabilities explained the problems he'd experienced all his life: the inability to write legibly, problems with spelling and numbers, difficulty telling left from right, halting speech, poor coordination in sports, lack of musical rhythmic skills, tendency to change his attention quickly from one thing to another.

As an adult he had known he wasn't stupid, despite having been told that in school. But for years, few others had taken the time to see beyond his limitations.

"He's lazy ... "
"He doesn't try ... "
"He's a daydreamer ... "

Like a cadre of disapproving companions, those evaluations escorted him into adulthood. Then the problems themselves had begun to take their toll. Inconsistent work performance had plagued him. Financial crises had recurred. Poor communication habits had bruised relationships.

Putting a Name to a Handicap

Finding a reasonable explanation for those difficulties had been very freeing. His personal burden had lightened considerably just knowing about his own unique character. There would never be an excuse for not trying.

But there was clearly a reason for not always succeeding.

Quickly scanning the brochures from the Orton Dyslexia Society, Ray put them aside to be read later. Looking at the rest of his mail, he ripped open a letter from an important Russian underground contact. A surge of excitement stirred within him.

The contact's note carefully explained some incidents that had recently occurred in the Soviet Union. There seemed to be a flicker of hope for some long-suffering Christians there. But no time could be wasted. Immediate action must be taken!

Lost in thought, Ray set the rest of the mail aside and headed toward the Canadian border crossing. *I've got to do something to help those people.* His mind raced ahead of his car.

When he got home, he knew he would find his desk in Vancouver piled with problems. He didn't have much money in the bank. And he definitely had some loose ends to tie up. What should he do first? He accelerated a little more and turned the radio dial, absently searching for a news broadcast.

A familiar sense of frustration began to annoy him. There was so much to do. Little seemed to be getting done. And everything took forever. Suddenly, like a somewhat faded photograph, the picture of an Irish schoolboy fixed itself in his mind.

Long ago, that child had lifted hope-filled blue eyes from a map in his geography book. On a daydream journey, he had gone wandering across unseen oceans, captivated by unimaginable landscapes on the far side of the world.

"The Fraser River, Canada," he had hesitantly whispered the words to no one but himself. "I expect I'll be going there some day. I don't know how I'll do it. But I will."

A smile tugged at the corners of Ray Barnett's mouth as he drove his car across the Fraser River. *Nothing is impossible. What else can be said about a life like mine?*

All at once he laughed aloud and spoke to Heaven. "Lord, it's true!

Some things are frustrating. Some things are difficult. Some things look completely hopeless. And people always have their own ideas about the way the job gets done. But with Your help nothing is impossible. Absolutely nothing."

EPILOGUE

FEBRUARY 2016

Thirty years have past since this story was first told, and the miracles—propelled by the hand of God and Ray's relentless drive, steadfast determination and refusal to take "no" for an answer—have continued to unfold in ways that even he couldn't have envisioned.

That first Choir effort in 1984, which Ray had hoped would raise enough money to build and support an orphanage in Uganda, instead led to a new calling—to use the gift of music to provide food, shelter, an education and hope to orphaned and destitute children throughout Africa.

The African Children's Choir, which has been going strong for more than three decades, has grown into an international sensation that has inspired audiences worldwide. The young Choir ambassadors have performed for dignitaries around the globe—including Queen Elizabeth, Prime Minister Gordon Brown, President George W. Bush, the United Nations, and the Clinton Global Initiative. They have also performed alongside music legends such as Paul McCartney, U2, Anne Lennox and Josh Groban, and have been featured in international symphonies, movie tracks and musicals.

By bringing their voices, resilience and message of hope to both small church audiences and large event goers throughout North America, Europe, Australia and Asia, the Choir has become a voice for the voiceless and has raised tens of millions of dollars that, to date, have providing healing and hope for tens of thousands of vulnerable children throughout Africa.

The African Children's Choir, facilitated by parent organization Music For Life, has provided an education for more than 52,000 children throughout Uganda, Kenya, Sudan, Rwanda, Nigeria, Ghana and South Africa. It has also directly impacted the lives of thousands of other vulnerable African children through music therapy and life skills training camps, Music For Life centers, and container shipments of food, clothing and supplies.

Over the years, Ray has personally signed on as legal guardian to more than a thousand children who have gone through the Choir program and have been fully supported by the organization to adulthood. With the support and love of the Music For Life staff and Daddy Ray, as he as affectionately called, many of the Choir children have earned their college degrees and have gone on to become doctors, attorneys, engineers, pastors, church leaders, journalists, teachers and relief workers in Africa—realizing Ray's full-circle vision of "Helping Africa's most vulnerable children today, so they can help Africa tomorrow."

Ray continues to keep an eye out for people being persecuted for their faith and has spearheaded international relief efforts whenever a crisis or need presents itself. Over the years, this has included rebuilding communities and schools for Christians displaced by the war in Southern Sudan—including the establishment of a teachers training college, which the organization still supports, and fifteen primary schools that have since been turned over to the new government of Southern Sudan—raising money for the Gisimba Children's Center in Rwanda to help care for and reunite children with living relatives after the horrific genocide there, and supplying windows for war-ravaged hospitals and schools in Albania

Ray is now looking at ways to help Christians in Syria, Afghanistan, Iraq and other parts of the Middle East who are facing imprisonment, torture and death by beheading because of their faith.

Friends in the West has also embarked on a new project, currently being piloted in South Africa, that provides youth mentoring and leadership training. The program complements the work Friends in the West is already involved in, adding another dimension to its work of raising awareness of Christians under threat, and encouraging prayer and practical support for the persecuted and displaced.

In his fifty years of Christian-based global human rights and relief work, Ray has learned to view his disabilities and struggles as gift. Because of his Dyslexia and Attention Deficit Disorder, Ray never stands still and is constantly taking on new, seemingly insurmountable relief and rescue challenges and then forging ahead and pushing others to join him until the situation is addressed. And his beginnings as a child who struggled with feelings of abandonment have driven him to do everything in his power to help persecuted Christians and suffering orphans and vulnerable children around the world to know that they aren't alone and haven't been forgotten.

Along with continuing to drive the Friends in the West mission with a new emphasis on the Middle East crisis, Ray is working on capturing his life story in his own words to inspire others to take action. His story is a testament to the power of faith, prayer and inner strength, and a reminder that regardless of the adversities we face, we all have the ability to move mountains if we choose to do so. The secret, says Ray, is to tackle it "one person at a time."

To reach Ray, please email him at Ray@friendsinthewest.com.

For more information on the African Children's Choir, please visit www.africanchildrenchoir.com.

For more information on the Friends in the West mission, please visit www.friendsinthewest.com.

CPSIA information can be obtained
at www.ICGtesting.com
Printed in the USA
FSOW01n1433280316
18533FS